Mike,
Preciate ya
Love ya,
Chip It

THE IMPACT OF INFLUENCE VOLUME 4

Coaches Using Their Influence To Create A Life Of Impact

Go get it!

By

Chip Baker

Co-authored by Powerful Influencers

2022

THE IMPACT OF INFLUENCE

COACHES USING THEIR INFLUENCE

TO CREATE A LIFE OF IMPACT

VOLUME 4

WRITTEN BY

CHIP BAKER

CO-AUTHORED BY POWERFUL INFLUENCERS

First Printing: 2022

ISBN: 978-1-7379501-5-8

Ordering Information:

Special discounts are available on quantity purchases by corporations, associations, educators, and others. For details, contact the publisher at the email listed below.

U.S. trade bookstores and wholesalers:
Please contact chipbakertsc@gmail.com.

DEDICATION

This book is dedicated to all of the people who have impacted our lives. We send a special dedication to our families and all of those who support us. We hope that this book will leave an everlasting impact and influence for many generations to come.

We are grateful for you!

PREFACE

Dear reader,

We hope that this book will be a blessing to you. In the following chapters, you will find the lessons that these powerful authors have learned throughout their journey to success. Our hope is that you will learn from these lessons and use them to help you operate more efficiently and effectively in your life.

Brief Description of Book

We all have been impacted by amazing influences in our lives. As such, we create an everlasting ripple effect by learning lessons from those that have affected us. When we apply those lessons, we can make our world a better place.

The Impact of Influence Vol. 4, Coaches Using Their Impact to Create a Life of Influence, is overflowing with wisdom from visionary author Chip Baker and other powerful coaches who have discovered their paths to success. They are influencing many and impacting generations. The inspirational stories within the pages of this book will inspire you to make a positive difference for those around you.

This empowering compilation highlights coaches that have faced challenges head-on, learned from each of them and pulled the blessings from the lessons. These coaches are now impacting our world in an amazing way.

TABLE OF CONTENTS

LIST OF AUTHORS IN CHAPTER ORDER

1. Chip Baker
2. Armando Jacinto
3. Charles Woods
4. Deidre Vasquez
5. Dereck Rush
6. Derek Koonts
7. Derrick Pearson
8. Greg Robinson
9. Hoss Tabrizi
10. Jason Haddock
11. Jessica Perez
12. Maggi Welham
13. Manny Trujillo
14. Royce Slechta
15. Tamika Newman
16. Taylor Cobb
17. Tyrone Void

COACHES INFLUENCE
Chip Baker

"Coaches have impacted me in a major way."
Chip Baker

A few years back I was at a sporting event with a friend who is a fellow coach. There was a student behind us that said "Hey Coach". We both automatically turned our heads in response to find out that he was not talking to us. He was talking to another coach that was sitting in our general area. The athlete got the attention of the coach that he was trying to talk to. I noticed that the athlete seemed to be in a panic but whatever the coach was saying seemed to calm him down. He eventually had a smile on his face. Observing this incident made me reflect on the impact that coaches have made on my life and in the lives of others. Coaches have impacted me in a major way. It made me think about all those coaches that I have had the privilege to play for, work under as an assistant, and work with. I have learned many great things from getting the chance to be in their presence. When reflecting on the great things they did I thought about the traits that stuck out in my mind and heart.

Consistency

The first trait the successful coaches had was consistency. Those great coaches were consistent! They were consistent in all their dealings with people, their mannerisms, and the way they followed rules. They were always respectful. They showed respect for everyone they came in contact with regardless of how they were approached. They were open and honest with everyone they encountered. Their demeanors were consistent and there was no guessing. You always knew what you were going to get from them. They were cool, calm, and collected until it was time to not be that. They knew when it was needed or not needed. With rules, they had integrity and followed them. They did the right thing at all times.

I worked for a coach that would say "Guys, I don't have many rules. There are just two rules. Rule Number 1…DO RIGHT! Rule Number 2…SEE RULE NUMBER 1…DO RIGHT!" This was funny but the coach preached it and lived by it.

Those great coaches were consistent in taking pride in doing the right thing and making child-centered decisions. One of my high school coaches showed me, by his actions, that it was important to have fun while working hard. He showed up to work every day with a smile while having high expectations for us. It was consistent, I knew what I was going to get from him each day.

Overboard

The second trait was that they went overboard. They went overboard to help others around them.

"If you help enough people get the things they want, you will get the things you want."
Zig Ziglar

They were great teachers. They taught everyone around them transferable skills that they could use to be successful in life. When they went overboard to help others around them, it promoted a growth mindset environment. Everyone they encountered learned something that made them better. In turn, they produced positive, productive, hardworking, successful citizens for our society with traits that can be carried on from generation to generation.

I have had many people in my life that have gone overboard to teach me many great skills. As I reflect, my little league and little dribblers coaches gave me hope. Hope that I could be successful in my life regardless of where I came from or regardless of any circumstances that one may feel could hold me back.

I first learned how to be a great teammate from my very first "head coach" that was in my house, my mother. She would go overboard with her clear precise orders which eventually taught me some lessons that have helped me tremendously. Growing up we would have to go to the laundry mat to wash our clothes. My mother (the coach) would call the play (give us our specific roles) then we would have to go execute our individual tasks so that the team would be successful.

I can hear her saying to me, "You gather all the dirty clothes from each room and bring them to the den". Then she would say to my sister, "You go get the detergent and gather up all the quarters around the house and bring it to the den". Then she would say to both of us "meet back here in the den in 15 minutes and separate the clothes by darks, lights, and whites. Ok....go!" This was kind of like her breaking the huddle into a "ready, break" voice. We would execute the play with persistence as we knew she had high expectations. We also knew how important the tasks were to the team. We also knew that there were consequences if we did not execute well, lol! We would tie the clothes up in big sheets, load them in the car and head out to the laundry mat. Her overboard coaching showed me that it was important to go overboard while coaching others with passion.

My junior high coaches introduced me to the importance of doing the fundamentals the right way. My high school coaches helped instill a great work ethic in me. My college coaches showed me the importance of planning and taking care of business.

Once I got into my career, some coaches gave me opportunities even when I did not feel worthy of deserving them. They believed in me and then coached me up to help me be successful. They would not let me fail. I continued to learn from and grow with coaches that were older and younger than me.

All of these skills I learned were transferable skills that I have used in my life to help me be successful. They have allowed me to go overboard and return that to help others.

Attain Knowledge

The third trait is they continued to attain knowledge. Not only were they happy with the coaching level they were currently in, but they also always gained more knowledge to help them be better at their craft. Knowledge is the key that opens the door to success. When a person has the knowledge and strives to attain more knowledge, their level of success is unlimited. As a teacher/coach, knowledge, can be sought in many ways. I have known teachers/coaches to read and research, communicate, compare with others in the profession, and observe others doing what they do. What made them great coaches is that they have taken that knowledge and used it effectively to benefit others. To know something is one thing, but to do something with it is a whole other thing. It is just like making a cake. One may have all the ingredients they need (eggs, flour, sugar, shortening, vanilla, baking powder, etc.) but not everyone can make a great cake. We must take the things we have learned (knowledge) and use them the right way to positively influence others. That is what great coaches do.

Confidence

The fourth trait they had was confidence. They were confident but not arrogant. They did a great job at what they did because they believed that they could. They had faith that they could defeat any challenge that was in front of them. That belief became infectious and contagious to all that were blessed to be around them.

"The secret of making something work in your lives is first of all, the deep desire to make it work; then the faith and belief that it can work."
Eileen Caddy

They did not go around bragging or boasting about their accomplishments. They enjoyed them and kept working hard to achieve more. It was like a quiet confidence. This type of trait just exuded through the staff and the students they were around and made everyone feel that they could do an effective job to benefit all.

Hand to Guide

The fifth trait is they were a hand to guide. They taught children to do the right thing and follow rules. Not only did they say it and demand it, but they also lived it.

"We're all destined to leave some kind of mark. We're all meant to walk a certain path, at a certain time, in a certain direction, for a certain purpose."
Denzel Washington- A Hand to Guide Me

They realized that they were here for a certain purpose, to walk that certain path. That purpose and path were to guide those around them the right way. They taught life lessons that children could take with them and use to be successful in their life. They understood that they were a part of a cycle. They took what they learned and used it to be a blessing to so many people. In turn, the people around them could take what they learned from them and use it to help someone else. It was an amazing cycle and created a positive ripple effect for generations.

C. O. A. C. H.

When I hear the word "coach" I don't just think of an actual person. I think about what the word means. Merriam Webster defines a coach as *one who instructs or trains or one who instructs players in the fundamentals of a competitive sport and directs team strategy.* In my mind, a coach is much more than that. To me a C.O.A.C.H. is one that is C-consistent, O- overboard, goes overboard to help others, A- attains knowledge, C- confident, and H- a hand to guide while also teaching fundamentals and strategies. My hope is that those of you reading this chapter can take some of the information and use it to help you be a better COACH. We all are coaches in some form or fashion. We are very fortunate to be in situations to coach others and have the opportunity to be a positive influence on many. We can all influence someone as they try to figure out their path. When we influence in an impactful manner, we don't need a curriculum to see that you are a part of the math. God bless you on your journey!

ABOUT THE AUTHOR:

See Lead Author's Bio in About the Author section.

OUR GAME
Armando Jacinto

Pre-Game

I hope that anyone who reads about my game as a coach will see your path to significance is not a unique or lonely path. As you read you will see how we all have similarities in our paths, and I hope this inspires you to continue your path. Please understand it is a process that only our maker knows when you will get what you asked of Him. Know this moving forward, the more effort and discipline you demonstrate the quicker your professional and personal success will happen because you will be ready when those opportunities present themselves to you.

My game began when I was in high school at Reicher Catholic High School in Waco, Texas. In all games, players have to do a pre-game before we start so that we are ready to play the game.

I will start by sharing my family's history. It will explain my path to significance. Our family history has always been one of impact in service-oriented professions from my paternal grandfather starting a church in Waco, Texas to my maternal grandparents being very influential through their work in the Boys Club, coaching, and education for over six decades.

As my high school years were coming to a close, I had chosen to major in business. I don't know why I choose business even though I was an all-state basketball player, loved sports, and came from a service-oriented family. As my graduation was approaching, I had a brief conversation with my high school basketball coach Richard Friedli. He asked what I was going to be my major. I responded business. To paraphrase, his response was, "Armando you are a great leader you would be a great coach." I decided at that time I was going to school to be a coach. Little did I know how this one conversation will set me on a path that as you read is going to be fulfilling, impactful, and significant.

I graduated from Baylor University in December of 1986. I grew up attending the Boys Club from age five which was directed by my grandfather. This is where I found my love for sports, particularly basketball. After my college graduation, I immediately had to make a decision that initiated my path forward. I was offered the opportunity to be the Unit Director of the Boys Club in Waco, a coaching position at University Middle School, and asked to enroll in the PE graduate program at Baylor University. After consulting with my family and remembering what my coach told me about what my future should be, and wanting to become financially independent, I chose to accept the coaching position.

As I watched games on television or in person, I remember thinking that when I become a coach that with my knowledge and experience as a player, I was going to win many championships. I realized early that no matter how much knowledge, passion, enthusiasm, or experience you have—you need players with talent. I also learned that you must be able to develop talent for teams to have success in the playing arena. Now for players to develop they have to trust that what you are teaching them is going to improve their chances of having an impact. That trust is developed by knowing you care for them as a person and not just how they can help you win games. That's where transformation occurs. As a coach your players are comfortable doing things a certain way. Our job as a coach is to get our players to understand that being

10

uncomfortable will lead to growth and development. My growth occurred by acquiring as much knowledge about the techniques and fundamentals of the sport and the positions I coached. I also spoke with other colleagues to develop more ways to teach the skills needed for development to occur. Reminder, still at this stage in my career have I mentioned anything about relationship building.

First Quarter

My coaching career began at University Middle School in Waco. I was excited to see what I could accomplish as a coach with my first group of players. I believed at that time to be a successful coach I focused on my player's mistakes to get perfection. What I realized immediately is that players responded better when there was a balance between praise and crucial guidance. I also realized that I had to fit my coaching to each player's personality. Some responded to guidance focus and others responded to praise-reward focus. The main thing I learned is that they responded not by how much you know but by how much you care. During my two and a half years at the middle school, I acquired a lot of knowledge with a variety of techniques, drills, practice plans, and strategies. This led to the moderate-to-high skill development of my players, but only moderate team success. This was puzzling to me because I observed the positive impacts I had on my players previously. In 1990, Leroy Coleman, the former head coach who recently passed away, asked me to move up to the high school staff due to the impact I had on athletes. He saw what I had done with the middle school teams and wanted me to bring my approach to the high school program.

As I began my first year at high school as a freshman football and assistant baseball coach, I wanted to impress the high school coaches and let them know that I belonged with them. So, I watched a lot of film and began to network with other coaches to learn all I could about technique, schemes, drills, and strategies.

During my first few years at the high school level, I immersed myself in the culture and acquired as much knowledge as I could to become a better technician and strategist regarding football and baseball which was my second sport. Our program was having mediocre to moderate success at the varsity level which still was puzzling to me and our staff because we were having success with our sub-varsity teams. During this time, I held animosity for other teams in our district and area that were having success at the varsity level. Still nothing about relationships. In my first year on the varsity staff, we had to only win one of our last two games to get into the playoffs and we came up short in both games. Then, I realized that with this group of seniors that I had coached since eighth grade, building the relationship was important. This is when it hit me that talent was there, I just needed to build a bond with the players to get over the hump and have the success on the field we both wanted. Even though the next senior class also came up short, our staff now together four years, could see it coming with our juniors. Those relationships were very solid! In our junior class, we broke through but lost in the first round. From that experience, the talent was there. We just needed to focus more on mental preparation. As I became more knowledgeable about the game, I also began to network with coaches about how they instilled those intangibles with their players, so the program sustained itself whenever obstacles presented themselves.

In 1992, after the previous year's success and having a great nucleus of returning juniors, we were expecting a great year on the field. We also as a staff had been four years together so we had built a bond as well and we all were purposely forging relationships with our players. In addition to becoming more confident with my knowledge, I sensed a change in the development of the players I coached. We experience the most success in 1992. We went 10-2 and bi-district champs but the best was yet to come.

By 1996, I made it a priority to improve as a coach by building relationships. I did that by having conversations with my players and getting to know them as people and not just players. That year we made it to the state quarter finals. The biggest reason for our success was leadership and chemistry, and we all just liked being around each other. The same year one of our former players was on our staff and his confidence in my knowledge inspired me to explore opportunities that would expand my abilities in the coaching arena.

Maurea Crain was his name. He asked if I ever thought of coaching at the college level and I told him I didn't feel my knowledge was at that level. He played at Iowa University and his team was Big ten champions. He told me I must have just as much or more knowledge than a lot of his college coaches. This conversation gave me the confidence to seek out leadership opportunities in coaching.

As I began to prepare myself to become a defensive coordinator and eventually a head coach, I did not truly know if I was doing the right things to be fully prepared for a coordinator position. In 1999 three people were put in my life by the man upstairs. Though I did not know it at the time, that helped put me on the path to fulfilling my career goals. They remain a part of my inner circle. Those three men were Brick Haley, Doug Fertsch, and John Williams. All of them aided in their own way. I would be remised if I did not recognize what I learned from them that helped give me direction. Coach Fertsch helped by exposing me to a network of coaches in the Texas High School Coaches Association (THSCA). His influence as the son-in-law of Eddie Joseph, got me in front of interview committees where I gained vast experience in the interview process. I acquired immense knowledge of techniques, and strategies, and learned how to have fun on the job. Big John Williams helped me see from a philosophical point and opened me up to see the big picture. I can confide in them when I need a perspective from someone not emotionally attached. For that, I will always be indebted to them. Moving on as our teams achieved great things on the field, I felt these accomplishments and experiences put me in a position to be qualified as a head coach.

Second Quarter

After twenty-five interviews and a change of schools, I became the head football coach and campus coordinator at Travis High School in Austin Independent School District (ISD). Here is where two other men would play a large part in the next phase of my career. These two men were Drew Sanders and Dr. Rene Garganta. When I came to Travis as DC, Coach Sanders was the head coach. He taught me organization and staying positive no matter how things were going on around us. I thank him for that. As for Dr. Garganta, my family and I will always be thankful he was the person who gave me my first head football coaching position and was instrumental in becoming an Assistant Athletic Director. My five years as head coach at Travis were very memorable. We were able to accomplish some things that were never done in school history which were five straight playoff appearances and winning the Battle of the Bell for the first time in twelve years. I want to also thank Ty Davidson who was the principal during my last four years as head coach. I thank him for supporting me and allowing me to pursue my athletic administrator career. I really enjoyed my time there not just because that is where I became a head coach and had huge success, but because of the relationships I built with the great staff, administration support, and players. Travis will always have a special place in my heart.

Third Quarter

The second half of my career is going to bring someone into my life who will profoundly change my life starting in 2014. As I progressed through my time at Travis, I saw the impact I had over an entire athletic program which entailed young men and women as well as a group of twenty plus coaches. Even though I loved the relationships I built I felt like an athletic administrator I could impact even a larger group of people. So, I began the process to apply for Assistant Director (AD) positions and came across a position that was open in Spring ISD. That brings me back to Coach Fertsch when I asked if he knew the AD in Spring ISD. He says he gave him his first job. Dr. Garganta, who coincidentally is in Spring ISD now as well, also knew the athletic director. I interviewed two times for the position. The next six years of my life are going to be in a different role but still impact more of the people's careers than the player's future. When I was hired as Assistant Athletic Director, I knew what my responsibilities were, but I needed to know what would be mine and why. As I spoke with the coaches in the district, they told me what the positives were and what needed to be addressed. At this point my why became clear, to encourage, enhance, equip, and inspire coaches as they work with student-athletes. I saw my younger self in a lot of the students, so I made it my purpose to help build and enhance those leadership skills to be great leaders. Being from another area I felt my primary purpose in this new job was to build trust with this new coaching staff. They did not know my background or experiences so I had to develop trust so they would allow me to lead them. I did this by delivering more than I promised and not promising more than I can deliver. This is the definition of integrity. I learned from my grandfather who to me is the most respected man I ever knew. As I stated during my six years as Assistant Athletic Director, we had tremendous success with all our teams winning over forty district championships, two hundred forty athletic scholarships, and over forty million in facility improvements. However, the accomplishment I am most proud of is the relationships I built with our coaches and athletes. This I feel was very important to the overall success of the athletic program.

Fourth Quarter

During my time as Assistant Athletic Director, Willie Amendola the AD always said to me when he decides to move on that I need to replace him to continue to fulfill our mission for the athletic program. So, in June of 2022, I officially became athletic director of Spring ISD and transitioned into the fourth quarter of my career. During this point, games are won, and games are lost. At this juncture in my game, I know I am on top. I don't have to look at the scoreboard because of the number of people who I have impacted. Although I am up in the game at this point, I know there are still more people I can impact because you play the game till the clock says 0:00. Those who still need to be impacted need my full attention. Up to this point I have broadcasted my take on the game. I now am going to speak about the people who made it possible to play this game (career) and be impactful to those I have coached and led. First and foremost is God. My blessings did not really begin until I stopped hating and put my career in His hands. Dominoes began to fall, and I realized through Him all things are possible. Secondly, my maternal grandparents, Paw and Mawmo. Paw showed me how to be a man, how to treat all people with value, and how to coach. Mawmo showed me the importance of family and it does not take a lot to go, first class.

What I learned from my mother, Linda, was how to survive. My parents divorced when I was in seventh grade. At that time my mother could not drive, did not possess any job skills, and only had a GED education. Knowing that she had to care for five children, she learned how to drive, got a job, and supported me and my four sisters. She was my biggest fan and she was always the first person in the stands to watch me play and coach. I asked her why she always came so early to my games, and she said I just love to watch you play and coach because I can see how you love what you do. I wished for anything I could get one more phone call from her. Next are my maternal uncles and aunts. They taught me how to play, the importance of education, and setting goals. My father Daniel, I learned about work ethic, and despite suffering a horrible work accident where he lost five fingers and almost a leg, not letting that keep him from living. To my sisters Tisha, Deanna, Dondy, and Patti my biggest cheerleaders. Thanks for all you have done for our parents when they needed you the most. My children, Tisha, AJ, and Velencia. They are my second biggest accomplishment. I am very proud of what they have become. They help me keep an open mind

I hope they are as proud of me as I am of them. Love them more than life itself. My grandchildren, Alashya and Jace. They are my world. There will be nothing I won't give or provide for them. I hope to live to see what they become. Last, but not least, my ride or die, Idell my wife. She is the nicest person in the world, the most patient (married to me for over thirty years), biggest accomplishment. I would still be an assistant coach if not for her. That is why the title of this chapter is Our Game. I would not be where I am as an administrator, coach, husband, and father without her being the best teammate ever. I owe her everything. That is why I have tried to help give her everything she has ever wanted because she deserves it all. To my wife's family, thank you for being some of my biggest supporters.

As I transition to the athletic director position, I want to thank all campus coordinators (high and middle school) and coaches. I am the administration for their support, the players, and our current staff that help us be the best and make my job easy and fun. Thank you, Coach Oliver. Elizabeth, Zelda, Monique, Joseph, and Blanca.

Post-Game Interview

In closing, I want to thank Coach Amendola I don't know if he remembers when he changed my life. If not let me remind him it's when he said, "How you doing?" I also want to thank Coach Garcia my mentor for always having my back. The following coaches Martinez, Horn, Harsh, Seaborn, Pena, Crayton, Riojas, Rauls, Hicks-Bailey, Stamps, and Crutchfield the Waco connection. I want to thank my newest team, the Hispanic Texas High School Football Coaches Association board of directors Castillo, Ojeda, Gonzales, Rodriguez, Vega, and Manning for selecting me as their president. I relish this position with great pride. I hope this game was as entertaining to read as it has been to play. I hope it inspires others to follow their dreams and go be impactful. Just remember to be significant in the game. It is about the relationships you nurture and not the plays.

ABOUT THE AUTHOR:

Social Media:
Email ajacinto@springisd.org

Armando Jacinto born in Waco, Texas attended Reicher High School. Graduated from Baylor University. Led basketball team to state finals was selected to Reicher Hall of Fame,1981 4A All-State Team, Waco Tribune 1981 basketball super Cen-Tex Team. Coached for 35 years. Coached at the following schools Waco University, Travis (head football coach-5 years, Spring ISD 7 years as 6 as Assistant AD, currently AD in Spring ISD. Current President of the Hispanic Texas Football Coaches Association serves on the IDEA committee for THSCA and the publications committee of THSADA. Married for 33 years have 3 children and 2 grandchildren.

A BETTER LIFE
Charles Woods

As a kid growing up, you have no idea where your life will take you.   You try to live your life through the experiences you go through and the influences that present themselves to you. The idea is that all of these experiences will be positive, great, and/or motivating, but we all know that is not how the world works. We will be confronted with challenges that we will have to overcome and decisions that we will have to make. Rather they are good or bad, right, or wrong these are our choices. Growing up in the neighborhood, I had no idea where my life was headed, but I did know there had to be something bigger and better than what I was experiencing. The days of peace and play were over and the time for focus and decision making was in front of me. School was my sanctuary; it was a place to get away from all the issues in everyday life that had begun to be overwhelming. I was learning things in school that was a good mix with my everyday neighborhood knowledge. These skills would help me survive in the real world, but there was the question of how would I continue my education? How would I be able to afford to continue learning after high school in an institution of higher learning? I had no idea how I would be able to attend a university, but I knew I had to figure it out. Little did I know my athletic ability, hard work, patience, and kind heart would afford me the opportunity to be a part of a life-changing experience.

It was my eighth-grade year, I was the starting quarterback for my eighth-grade football team at Travis Junior High School. This is unbelievable!!! I originally played football because my close friends were playing. They loved football and were joining the team, so why not? I might as well join the team also. In my seventh-grade year, the first year I played organized football, I played defense and strong safety, and in our defense because of my speed all I did was line up next to the nose track and blitz the A gap. A little football lingo for my football peeps. That year I also enjoyed playing basketball. I actually enjoyed basketball more than football, so for me to be named the quarterback of my team, in my eighth-grade year was a total shock. I owe this life-changing opportunity to my eighth-grade football coach, Coach Allen Woodum. He saw something in me that I didn't see. This coach believed in me and my abilities. I was a part of a team, and I became not only a strong teammate but a strong leader. Long story short, this was a great experience. We went undefeated but more importantly, I was learning skills that could support me throughout my life. These skills were always inside of me, athletics helped bring those skills out and fine-tune them. Those skills are defined by the word GREAT. Great is always what I strive to be and what I promote for others. For me, GREAT means the following:

Grateful

- For every day you get to open your eyes and have the opportunity to get better.
- For the individuals that came before you and made it possible for you to have these opportunities.
- For everyone that took the time to support you on your journey.

Resilient

- Never let your trials and tribulations stop you from accomplishing your goals.
- Keep pushing yourself to be the best vision of yourself.

Energy

- Your energy controls your productivity.
- Your energy will determine your outcome.
- Positive energy will drive your success and keep you motivated throughout your process.

Accountable

- There is no other individual that can hold you more accountable than yourself. Take on the challenge and monitor yourself.
- Be willing to allow someone to take on the responsibility of being your accountability partner when needed.

Trust

- Make sure you are exhibiting characteristics and actions that will build a foundation of trust. -Be willing and execute the ability to believe and rely on others.
- Always be firm but fair. Lead with a kind heart and care for others, but the expectations are the expectations.

That eighth-grade year was monumental in preparing me for my immediate future. I was now in high school and the thought of going to college and playing sports was starting to cross my mind. My academics were not bad, but I could absolutely do better. I let different outside issues get in the way of me meeting my true academic potential, but my ninth-grade year playing football was even better than my eighth-grade year. I got a little bigger and faster and the game was clearer than ever. In the first game of the year, I moved from quarterback to running back because at that time that was the best move for the team. That year I led all freshmen in rushing yards, kickoff return yards, and touchdowns. I also attempted to play a little defense at cornerback, emphasis on the word attempted. I was okay at cornerback but in my eyes, I was a much better offensive guy, well that's what the stats said. There was actually a little talk about me moving up to varsity. How true that was or not I really don't know. That could have been just some of the talk from the upper-class men that saw the success I was having on the freshman level or it could have come from the coaches. I never really gave it too much thought. I did get a chance to run the 4x100 meter relay on varsity my freshman year. I did not see that coming at all. Our head track coach, Coach Robert Collett, had faith in my abilities even when I was an inexperienced little freshman. That was an amazing experience that set the tone for my future. Athletics was creating a space for me to focus my energy in a positive way instead of focusing on the negative things that were going on in my home life. Athletics was slowly opening a door for me to get out of my unwanted situation. All I had to do was keep working hard, keep focused on my goals, keep treating people right, and keep leading with empathy and a kind heart. I started understanding that my future was in my hands. Not all young men of my color have or take advantage of this type of opportunity.

My sophomore summer was over and it was time to go to work. Me and every kid in the state of Texas that played football were starting two-a-day football practice. It was hot and the days were long, but we looked forward to these days. I received a big unexpected surprise on the first day of practice, I was invited to practice with the varsity football team. Now rewind to my ninth-grade year, I was a better offensive player than a defensive player, in my mind, but I was invited to varsity practice as a defensive player. This did not make sense to me. I was actually practicing at cornerback. I did not think I had a good year at cornerback my freshman year. Really it didn't matter, I was going to put in one hundred percent effort and see what happened. On the second day of practice, I was the first player in the defensive secondary film room and noticed my name on the depth chart with the first-team defense at the right corner. Wow, I couldn't believe it. Maybe there was a future for me at cornerback. Maybe I wasn't as bad at defense as I thought. Then it all hit me. It was starting to make sense. This is why the varsity defensive back coach always came to the freshman home games and ALWAYS coached me up at corner. He was also my freshman basketball coach and he would leave the weight room open for me after basketball practice so I could lift weights. He would also come to see me run track or ask me how I did when he could not make the track meets. Coach Chris Massey had a plan for me, one that I had no idea about. He saw something in me that I did not see. That is all a kid like me needed. No one was going to outwork me and now I had someone that is giving me a chance to play on Friday nights. The door of opportunity had just opened a little more. About five games into the session, I received a typed letter from the University of Texas. Again, this was a typed letter, nothing personally written or nothing special about this letter, but it had my name on it. This was the final piece. I knew this was my path. I knew I was going to college and getting a college degree with the help of football. This was my way to a better life.

My Senior year is here, and things are working out for me to my surprise. Even with all the things that were happening with the team. We did not have a lot of success as a team. Coaches changed, we got a new head coach my junior year and new coaches at all positions. My original defensive back coach had moved on to a different school and I had to start over. This new coach was actually on staff before the coaching change. He was an offensive varsity coach that I was really unsure about, but he ended up being my guy as well. He coached receivers the previous year and was always on our secondary about staying off the receivers, but we quickly learned that was his passion for the game and the care that he had for his players. The biggest impact was him taking the time to build relationships with the defensive secondary and earning our trust. I had and have nothing but respect for Coach Greg Poole, now Dr. Greg Poole. I can truly say I had the pleasure of being coached by some amazing coaches during my public school experience. From those experiences I was blessed to have several choices of universities to pick from, starting with junior colleges, HBCUs, Division 1AA, and Division 1A Universities. Things fell in place and on national signing day I chose to sign a five-year football scholarship to the University of Southwestern Louisiana, today known as the University of Louisiana at Lafayette. How did a kid like me get so lucky? Maybe this hard work thing pays off. Two goals accomplished. I graduated high school and received a full scholarship to a university.

Thank you Coach Doug Fertsch for seeing something in me and putting me on your list of recruits.

Walking on the practice field for my first day of two a day practice in college, the heat and humidity was energy-draining, and believe it or not this made some young players change their mind about playing college football. These players ended up going home due to the mixture of heat, humidity, and being home sick. Neither one of those situations was going to ruin this experience for me. This was an exciting time in my life and an experience of a lifetime. I had just opened a new chapter in my life and there is no way I was going backward. In my first year of college football, I was redshirted but my defensive back coach kept me prepared knowing that I was one injured cornerback away from getting the call up to the travel quad. We competed in the Big West Conference which meant we had a chance to win a conference championship and go to a bowl game. The football program did not resign a contract with the Big West Conference and our program went independent. Independent meant we were not in a conference, which made it hard on the program. Wins were hard to come by, so bowl games were a distant memory. I watched so many coaches come and go and our program took a pounding. It was rough at times, but my goal stayed the same. I would not let this change the plans that I had for my life. It was bigger than me and this moment in time. I had a future to prepare for. I would stay the course and continue to work hard every day, but boy was I tested.

College football was like having two jobs along with classwork. This took a little getting used to, but I was up to the challenge. I saw scholarship and walk-on athletes come and go, failing out of school or going home because they were not mentally prepared and/or did not know how to adjust to change. My thoughts remained the same, this was a great opportunity and there was no turning back. These next four to five years could make a huge difference in my life. The challenge was easy. The choices were hard.

Unlike a lot of the kids that looked like me or came from neighborhoods like mine, my dream was not to be in the NFL or NBA. My dream was to have a better life. To go to college and be an engineer or something similar. I was going to use football to get a degree. Don't get me wrong, I would put everything into being the best athlete I could be. The difference was it didn't stop there. I would also be the best student I could be. I would not let a FULL ride scholarship go to waste. I knew that in every game there was a fifty percent chance that we would win or lose. Someone had to lose. I never let the wins and losses dictate my life. I made sure that I was prepared and everyone around me was prepared as best as they could be. There was never a time when I did not leave everything that I had on the field. I owed this to football because football took care of me. I successfully earned a bachelor's degree in Industrial Technology and was called back to be a defensive graduate assistant football coach at my university and earned a master's degree in Engineering and Technology Management. Thank you, Coach Mike Doherty, Coach Gary Bartel, Coach Nelson Stokley, Coach Jerry Baldwin, Coach Tyke Tolbert, Coach Chris Gannon, Coach Marion Hobby, Coach Carey Bailey, and all the other coaches that took the time to pour into me. I learned a lot from the coaching, the conversations, the examples (good or bad), and the care and love. Everything a young man like me needed.

It's amazing that an individual can go through so many things in life and they never know or understand the true impact that they had on others. I am grateful that I was able to let several coaches that had an impact on my life know how important they were in my journey and how grateful I am for them. While having these conversations I found out from several coaches that I had an impact on their lives as well. I made their jobs easier and/or helped advance their careers. This opened my eyes to something that I never thought about. This was a great example of how impact can come in all shapes and sizes, ages, and races.

I am extremely grateful for having the opportunity to play the sport that I learned to love at the collegiate level and use this opportunity to better my life by successfully receiving two college degrees. This would not have happened without the coaches that were placed in my life. We are much more than the sports that we played and my coaches made that clear. We are student-athletes, notice the word student is first. Without my coaches and the extra time that they put into me, there is no telling where I would be. Yes, I had dreams beyond my neighborhood, but those dreams came more and more clear with the support of those coaches that crossed my path.

Coaching doesn't just occur in sports. Coaches are everywhere and in every field. These are the individuals that support others. The individuals that want to see everyone around them and/or the organization be successful. Connect with the individuals that believe in you and can support your goals. Be a sponge and soak up as much information as possible. Work hard and continue to work hard. Your path might not be easy but the journey is worth it. Continue to believe in yourself. If you don't believe it, how can you expect others to believe it? My life came full circle. Next up for me was the title Coach.

ABOUT THE AUTHOR:

Social Media:
IG @ullgrad1911
FB @charles.woods.1612
Email ullgrad1911@hotmail.com

Charles Woods is a public-school building principal that leads with a positive mindset and a drive to support educators as they effectively support young scholars to increase their academic outcomes and develop strong social-emotional behaviors. Charles has nineteen years in public education, nine years as a classroom teacher and football coach, six years as a head boys track coach, five years as an assistant principal, and five years as a building principal.

Charles has an M.S. in Engineering and Technology Management and a B.S. in Industrial Technology from the University of Louisiana at Lafayette. Where he received a full athletic scholarship and a graduate assistant scholarship. Charles was the team captain of the football team during his senior year at the University of Louisiana at Lafayette. He returned to the University after his senior year to be a graduate assistant football coach.

Charles Woods is a Best-Selling Author for his collaborative work in The Impact of Influence Volumes 1 and 2. He is also a Coach, Mentor, and Motivational Speaker.

Charles is the husband to Celena Woods and stepfather to Courtney and Chelsea Greer.

His certifications include:
Superintendent Certification
Principal Certification
EC -12 Special Education Certification
NCI certified instructor
Rice University Leadership Partner's Executive Education Academy

There is no other profession that gives me the opportunity to impact lives like public education. I did not choose this path; this path chose me. I will continue to be a servant leader to those in my care and to those that choose to work with me. I am grateful for this opportunity to make a difference and mold our young scholars.

Quotes:

Don't assume anything and be prepared for everything!!!
Think GREAT!!!, Do GREAT!!!, Be GREAT!!!
Do Better, Be Better!!!
The grass is never greener, some grass needs more water.
I live to serve; I don't serve to live.
Don't be a product of your environment, make your environment be a product of the positive you!!!

UNLIMITED
Deidre Vasquez

As an athlete, I have been blessed to have had many amazing experiences during my time competing in the sports realm. Many, if not all, of these experiences, were made possible because I had a strong foundation of support. At this point in my life, I realize how vital that collective group of supporters was to me. I am beyond thankful for the people that contributed so much.

I went through a rough patch back in junior high. I was cut from the basketball team in seventh grade. Then, I came back the next year and made the eighth-grade team merely to find out that I would be able to play in only the first game of the season. My Dad was an engineer and had accepted a job transfer to Nacogdoches, Texas. Over the winter break, our family moved almost two thousand miles away. Talk about a culture shock! We were very close to our family back home and now it was just the four of us in a new state with a much different climate, in a new town with new faces and new accents. Thankfully, there were sports! Those, for the most part, were the same as I knew them to be back in Ohio. Soon after moving into our new house, it was time to enroll in school. I am naturally a shy person, and I really was back then, so going to a new school was beyond intimidating. At my new school, they had an athletic period during the school day. This was not how it was in Ohio, but I remember thinking it was such a cool concept, especially for me and the love that I had for sports. Athletics was the first period of the day and they were still in basketball season. I remember that first practice and going for it. After being cut from the team in seventh grade and leaving after the first game in eighth grade, I was not going to let this opportunity be interrupted by fear of being in a different environment. Besides, being on that court was my comfort zone. I ended the school year with track and then joined the local softball league.

In high school, I played volleyball, basketball, and softball and ran distance races in track and field. Whenever I was asked what my favorite sport was, I would often respond with whatever sport was "in-season" at the time. Well, except for track. It was never a favorite. I participated in track because I had a strong will to win and compete. I used it to help me improve as an athlete in other sports. Running wasn't fun to me but winning a race or medaling in a race was the part that I loved most. I also loved knowing that I gave it my all and pushed myself during the competition; that in itself was a victory for me especially when I ran a personal record (pr). It made all the pain that I felt in practice and during the race worth it. In my freshman year of high school, I made regionals in the 1600m, and from that point forward I was locked into competing on the track team. I remember wishing my races were not running four and eight long boring laps on a track, but that's what they had to be for me to have my best chance of winning. My true loves were softball, volleyball, and basketball.

My family was my rock-solid foundation. There wasn't pressure from my parents to achieve. There were never any negative comments after my less-than-successful performances. I was naturally extra tough on myself. They could tell I was disappointed already, so I would get the "you will do better next time" or "you are human and can't expect to play perfectly" votes of confidence. My mom was my biggest cheerleader. She would give me pep talks constantly about how I could do anything I put my mind to. I could always hear her voice over every other from the stands of even the loudest venues. They didn't have sports for girls back when she was in school, so she knew how much of a blessing it was for me to have these opportunities. She experienced great joy from seeing me doing things that she didn't have the chance to do as a youngster. My dad was always there to help me work on my skills, but most of the time it was me asking him to help me improve. I interrupted many of his Sunday afternoon naps to rebound for me or play burn-out in the backyard. He was also the one who tried to help me control my temper when I would miss shots, strike out, or make a mistake of any kind. Thankfully, I became level-headed like him as I matured. As I mentioned earlier, it was just us living in Texas so we had to be there for each other. My brother and I would compete at everything. We would wrestle each other until one of us would leave the room mad and crying. We would have sit-up contests, foot races, and the most intense ping pong games you could imagine just to name a few. We would make up games and then battle just to see who could proclaim winner status. Our competitive natures were mirror images of each other. If a contest was involved, there was never a dull moment between him and me.

High school sports are where I encountered wonderful people outside of my family that set me up for the sports successes in my life. These remarkable people were my coaches. They were the perfect blend of an array of personalities. They each knew how to hold their athletes to a high standard while being supportive role models. I could tell that they were passionate about coaching and impacting the lives of their athletes. Coaching was not about them. It was about the teenagers that they poured time and energy into, their teams, and their athletes. This is where I felt the most impact from my coaches. Being a multi-sport athlete was very important to me. Collectively, this group of educators, completely supported me in this venture all four years of high school. I never felt pressure about not being in the other coach's off-season program. Comments were never made to make me second guess my decision to be a part of four athletic programs or to make me think I was going to "get behind the others" because I wasn't with their specific program year-round. On the contrary, there was complete support! Total encouragement from all of them no matter what the season was. They each made it a smooth transition to move from one sport to the next. I remember how heavy that basketball felt every year after volleyball season. Surely, I was a little rusty those first couple of practices transitioning from one sport to another. Instead, they allowed me to work through the kinks and in turn thrive as an overall high school athlete.

I am truly grateful for those coaches and feel like they were the cultivator of every good athletic experience I had since being their athlete. They allowed me to follow my heart and blossom in all playing fields. Today, so many young athletes are expected to specialize in one sport. Parents and coaches are usually the ones influencing those decisions. Coaches are consumed with the "it's all about me and the success of my program" mindset. Parents are driven by that coveted athletic scholarship carrot that dangles out in the future and the "look how good my kid is" way of thinking. In most cases, the athlete's decisions are made for them. They are not encouraged to participate in multiple sports because they "could get hurt" or miss out on an "amazing off-season program and bonding time with teammates". I wish coaches and parents would take their personal agendas out of it and instead trust that their athletes will grow even more when given new experiences and situations to learn and work through.

My way of seeing it is that you only get to be in high school once in your life and when you are there you should have the chance to make the most of it. Learn the most you can learn. Become as well-rounded as you possibly can. It was priceless for me to have the chance to learn from four times as many coaches. Coach Judy Justus taught me to believe in myself even when faced with tough challenges. She poured her heart and soul into every practice and every game. I knew she wanted to push us to be the best volleyball and softball players and team we could possibly be. Coach Gordon Fountain brought so much joy to the basketball court while teaching the game. Don't get me wrong, he hated losing just as much as I did (my senior season was a tough one on the win/loss record), but I remember his unique laugh. It was okay to laugh when something funny happened in practice or was said or done on the bus or in the huddle. I truly believe he loved coaching and cared about his athletes. Coach Johnnie Simpson was such a supportive leader. She had to have a lot of trust in me. She knew that to have me compete at the track meet on Saturday there would always be softball on Friday night. Every day at school I would get the track workout from her to do during the athletic period and then after school, I was committed to softball practice/games. Coach Pam Sears was not one of my head coaches but was very impactful in that I saw how she could be an effective math teacher and coach at the same time. Each one of them showed me how they could be a great coach and get the most from their athletes in different but supportive ways.

With all the selfless acts from my coaches, I was allowed to thrive in multiple competition settings which spurred my academic achievements in the classroom. I had a reason to do my best in my academics too! Even though I played multiple sports in high school, it did not interfere with my ability to sign an athletic college scholarship. I played collegiate basketball for four years on an athletic scholarship (played for an exceptional coach then too). I had such a wide range of experiences from competing in many athletic settings that I was prepared for the challenges and demands of being a collegiate athlete. There was no risk of burn-out because I was allowed to keep the competitive flame burning during those high school years. I never got tired of the grind. Every game was a blessing and an opportunity, not a job/task or something I felt I had to do.

I have taken what I learned from my amazing coaches to formulate myself as the coach that I am today. I'm confident that they are responsible for helping me choose my career path. I knew I wanted to be to others what they were to me. I am beyond blessed to have had the privilege to be a part of each of their athletic programs and realize the impact they had on the athletic foundation of my life. The best part of this is that I get to pass what they instilled in me on to my athletes! I know the importance of teenagers being involved in multiple activities in high school. I know the value of being able to learn from multiple leaders. I know the value of being able to be involved in different venues. As a coach and leader of female athletes, I know they will be the most empowered when they have a multitude of experiences to grow from.

ABOUT THE AUTHOR:

Social Media:
FB @deidrevasquez
Email dvasquez@conroeisd.net
Twitter @vasquez_deidre

Deidre Vasquez is a successful high school basketball coach and math teacher. She enjoys working with teenagers and helping them realize they can achieve greatness both on the court and in the classroom.

THE POSITIVE IMPACT A FATHER AND MOTHER CAN HAVE IN A CHILD'S LIFE

Dereck D. Rush

"Train up a child in the way he should go and when he is old he will not depart from it"
PROVERBS 22:6

"Today's children are different."

This year is going to be my twenty-third year in public education. I'm currently the Director of Athletics for the Bryan Independence School District located in Bryan/College Station, Texas. Too often I hear this coming from a Teacher, Coach, or Administrator. Today's Children Are Different. I think that statement couldn't be further from the truth. Reflecting on that statement, I do believe that the influence and impact a father or mother can have on a child's life has changed, therefore making today's children different in so many ways.

Growing up in Philadelphia, Mississippi, my life was no doubt impacted by my father and mother. I was one of nine siblings, growing up on Bennett Street, living in a three-bedroom/two-bathroom house. As one could imagine with 11 people living in a three-bedroom/two-bathroom house, we had many challenges. This didn't stop my father and mother from always providing for us. They gave us the things we needed to survive in life, not the things we sometimes wanted just because. In our home on Bennett Street, the lessons my siblings and I learned from our parents played a huge role in our adult lives.

My mother, Mary Alice Rush, was born and lived in Mississippi her entire life. She was one of two siblings. As I think back over the life of my mother, she was a woman with a caring and forgiven spirit. She was a woman of faith who believed in the power of prayer. Since my father was traveling most of the time preaching, pastoring, and working trying to make ends meet for his family, Mother was often left raising nine children on her own. As a housewife, her service in the community was well known. I remember her driving many elderly women and neighbors in the community to the grocery store to purchase food like it was yesterday. She was not a woman of many words, but you always knew where she stood on issues, and she was not afraid to set seven boys and two girls straight on any problems that may have affected our home.

Mom taught us the value of respecting one another and respecting other people. She did not spare the rod. One of the things that I will always remember from her was: She would often say "Do with what you have until you can do better." This meant, do your very best and make the very best out of the small things God has blessed you with, and when He blesses you with more, be grateful and make the very best out of that as well. Furthermore, take care of the things God has blessed you with, big or small. My mother passed away my senior year in high school. I remember that fall evening in October like it was yesterday. I was sitting in the choir stands listening to my father teach the word of God, when my mother became sick at church and had to be rushed to the hospital. Later that week, she passed away. At the end of the day, my mother was truly committed to making sure her nine children had the character and Christian values to be successful in this crazy world.

My father, Rev. A.C. Rush, was also born and lived in Mississippi his entire life. He was the youngest of twelve siblings. Dad and mom grew up in the State of Mississippi during the height of racism and oppression toward black people. When I think about my father's life, I think of a servant and leader, one who dedicated this life to helping others. My father was a preacher and pastor for over 50 years in the State of Mississippi. He was also a civil rights activist helping other black people across the State of Mississippi fight against racism, oppression, injustice, and poverty. My father was the first black person to serve on the Philadelphia High School Board of Directors. As I recall growing up in that three-bedroom, two-bathroom house with eleven people, my father was the only breadwinner in the house. He worked many jobs and wore many hats providing for his wife and nine children. The impact my father had on us over the ninety years he spent on this earth was worth more than gold. He modeled to his seven sons and two daughters the importance of providing for his family, the value of hard work, the value of helping others and the foundation of believing in God, and the philosophy of putting God first in everything you do. He also taught us the importance of getting a quality education and a quality Christian education as well. As I sit here reminiscing over the impact my father played in molding me into the husband, father, coach, and friend I am today, I can't thank God enough for the powerful impact he had on my life. My father passed away in July 2021 at the age of 90.

Now that you know the characteristics of my parents and the powerful values they instilled in me and my siblings, I would like to share with you how these values impacted my life; Both as a young man growing up in Mississippi, as a division one college football, and Head Football Coach and Athletics Director in the State of Texas.

Like a lot of states and cities across the United States of America, high school football on a Friday night is a way of life. It was no different in the city of Philadelphia, Mississippi. All six of my brothers played the game of football and from 1978 until 1995, a Rush brother played on the Philadelphia High School football team. Before I became a player for the Philadelphia High School football team, I watched five of my brothers play the game of football with commitment, effort, enthusiasm, and encouragement. They competed with these values every time they played the game on Friday nights. So, by the time my younger brother and I made it to high school, my older brothers had created a reputation around the city of Philadelphia in which people called us the "hard-hitting Rush boys". I recall growing up not being able to attend all their games in person. I would listen to the games on the radio with my mother and other siblings eating baked peanuts cooked by my mother before the game started. The broadcaster would paint a picture of what was taking place in each play, and with a tone of voice that seemed to draw you toward the game. I would always imagine myself playing high school football one day and making my brothers proud, upholding the reputation of the "hard-hitting Rush boys" and beating our cross-town rival Neshoba Central.

During the Fall of 1988, my freshman year, I started on the Varsity football team. I remember traveling to Europa, Mississippi for my first varsity football game. We won that game and launched a great reputation for Philadelphia High School football over the next four years. I truly believe the impact my parents played in my life helped me reach that goal of playing high school football as a freshman. That humble spirit that both of my parents possessed and instilled in me and my siblings helped us achieve many goals in life.

It is often said that in life there are two guarantees that will happen to you. Number One: You will be faced with adversity, and Number Two: You will die. How you handle those challenging life experiences will have an overwhelming effect on the success you have in life. I faced many life-changing experiences and challenges in my senior year in high school. That year was a roller coaster of ups and downs. During the fall of October of my senior year, my mother passed away and that seemed to turn my world upside down. During the winter of November in my senior year, my team and I won a state championship in football. It was a roller coaster feeling. During the winter of December, I found out from my high school counselor that I was short one math class to qualify and be accepted into a division one college. I only had one more semester in high school to get that done. I had to get this done while taking an algebra class and a corresponding geometry class during the same semester. Also, during this time, I was being recruited by almost every division one college in the nation. During the winter of February of my senior year, I experienced a series of roller coaster events. We won a state championship in basketball. Another roller coaster feeling. During the spring of April and May, I completed my geometry class and signed a scholarship to play football for Mississippi State University in Starkville, Mississippi. During the summer of June, I was invited to play in the Mississippi/Alabama All-Star football game and was also invited to play in July. After playing in the Mississippi All-Star Game, I injured my ACL, and that required surgery. Also, one week before reporting to Mississippi State University, I was told by the university that I would not be able to attend because the SEC didn't accept correspondent classes.

As I reflect on my senior year with all the highs and lows that came into my life, I have no doubt in my mind that the powerful values my father and mother instilled in me through their everyday actions helped me persevere through these experiences. Because of the powerful value of never quitting anything in life, I went on to attend Mississippi College, a division two college in Mississippi. During my freshmen year at Mississippi College, I couldn't participate in football because of my knee injury. So, I spent my freshmen year rehabbing my knee from the ACL surgery. During my redshirt freshmen football year at Mississippi College, I was named an All-GSC Linebacker. Going into my sophomore year at Mississippi College the university dropped down to division three and that meant they would not be offering athletic scholarships anymore. Because of that adverse situation, Mississippi State University reached out to me and offered me another football scholarship. I went on to have a great career at Mississippi State

University and in my senior year, I was named an honorable mention ALL-SEC linebacker.

After graduating from Mississippi State University, I moved to Odessa, Texas in pursuit of a career in teaching and coaching. I was offered a job as a teacher/coach at The Academy of Ector, a junior high school that feeds into Odessa High School. After two years of teaching and coaching at the junior high level, I quickly moved up the career ladder, making stops at Odessa High School, Midland Christian High School, John Tyler High School, and Conroe Oak Ridge High School. I spent five years at John Tyler as the Campus Coordinator/Head Football Coach and in Conroe at Oak Ridge High School. Again, the influence and impact my father and mother had on me growing up prepared me to move twelve hours from my hometown of Philadelphia, Mississippi in pursuit of a successful career in the State of Texas.

My parent's influence, playing the game of football at a very high level, and coaching the game of football in the State of Texas have given me the opportunity to meet a lot of great people in my life. In over twenty-two years in the educational field, thirteen as a head football coach has allowed me to influence and impact a lot of young people's lives and that is something I do not take for granted. I have always felt like being a head coach was like pastoring a church. As I mentioned previously, my father was a pastor and preacher for over fifty years. As a pastor of a church, you are trying to get different people with different attitudes and backgrounds on the same page and moving in the same direction, which is serving the Lord. As a head football coach, you are doing the same thing, trying to get different young men with different attitudes and different backgrounds on the same page of doing things right on and off the field and winning football games as a team.

Going into my second year as a head coach, I wanted to build our football program on some type of motto or words that would impact our young men's lives on and off the football field. Something they could remember after their playing days were over and something that would help them be successful in the real world.

So, that summer before the season started, I reflected on my life and the things my parents taught me growing up on Bennett Street and how those values impact my success in my life. I came up with five words from my life experiences that my football team could apply to their life daily. Even when going through adversity, there was no doubt in my mind that they would be successful at anything in life. As a coaching staff at John Tyler High and Conroe Oak Ridge High School, we preached these five words to our football teams year around. We had these five words posted throughout the field house. In the offseason, our players had to put these words into action every day during their drills. We wanted these words to become a habit, just like walking is a habit. When you are walking around, do you think about walking? The answer is NO because it is a habit. That is how we wanted those five words to be in our young men's lives daily.

So, because of the talent we had and the belief our young men have in those five words, we were very successful at John Tyler High School and Oak Ridge High School. Even now as an Athletic Director, I put these five words into action on a daily basis in the administrative world. If you are an athlete, teacher, coach, businessman, doctor, or just going through some type of life challenge, put these words into action every day and you will be successful.

1. Committed
The first step in being successful in anything in life is you must be committed even when things are not going well.

2. Effort
You must show effort. That is one thing in life as an individual you can control. Your effort cannot be coached, it must come from a place of want and commitment to whatever it is that you are doing.

3. Enthusiasm
To be successful at something you must like it and be excited about what you are doing. Knowing at the end of that day things will work out.

4. Encouragement

No matter what your life goals and accomplishment are, just remember you cannot do it on your own. You will need help and encouragement from someone along the way. Sometimes you must encourage yourself. Encouragement gives you the strength to fight on.

5. Compete

Life is all about competing. If you are interviewing for a job, fighting a sickness, playing in a football game, or just going through some type of adversity you must compete to be successful.

The positive influence and impact my parents had on me growing up truly have helped mold me into the man I have become. There's nothing more powerful on this earth than the influence of a parent on their children. So, if you put God first and put these five words into action every day, success will be around the corner.

ABOUT THE AUTHOR:

Social Media:
IG @DereckRush
FB @DereckRush
Email dereck.rush@bryanisd.org

Dereck Rush Assistant Athletic Director with Bryan ISD. Dereck Rush is a native of Philadelphia, Mississippi. He has a wife, Angel, and two daughters Trinity and Addisyn. He holds a Bachelor's Degree in Fitness Management and a Minor in Business Administration from Mississippi State University. He also has a Master in Educational Leader from Grand Canyon University and a (CAA) Certified Athletic Administrator from the National Interscholastic Athletic Administrators Association, Indianapolis, IN. Dereck Rush was an All-SEC-Linebacker for Mississippi State University. He started his coaching career at Mississippi State University as a student coach. He spent two years as an Asst. Coach at Ector Junior High School in Odessa Texas, and three years as a Defensive Coach at Odessa High School, Odessa Texas. He served one year as the Defensive Coordinator at Midland Christian High School in Midland, Texas. He spent the next 9 years at John Tyler High School in Tyler, Texas. He served four years as the Defensive Coordinator and five years as the Head Football Coach/Campus Athletic Coordinator. As the Head Football Coach/Campus Athletic Coordinator at John Tyler High School, the team won four district championships and made it to the quarter-finals twice and semi-finals once. After his tenure at John Tyler High School Dereck became the Head Football Coach/Campus Athletic Coordinator for Conroe Oak Ridge. The team makes it to the playoffs four years and during his second year at Conroe Oak Ridge, the team started the season 7-0, and the next year they started the season 6-0. Coach Rush was named East Texas Coach of the year during his stay at John Tyler High and Montgomery County Coach of the year during his stay at Conroe Oak Ridge High School. Dereck Rush is going into his third year as the Asst. Athletic Director with Bryan ISD.

DON'T STOP BELIEVING
Derek Koonts

I can vividly remember waking up early on Saturday mornings when I was a kid, loading up the family car, and rushing over to my grandparent's house. I would typically ride with my grandfather in his VW Bug. We would fly down Nob Hill, get on the road and end up in a small town somewhere in Ohio to cheer for my uncle Punkie and the Muskies of Muskingum College. My uncle played defensive back and would have his name called repeatedly for making tackles or defending a pass play. Uncle Punkie played hard and was a great teammate. I say that because that is what his teammates would say about him after the games. Sometimes, we would go to his dorm room after his home games, and I thought that was the coolest thing in the world. I loved spending time with my family and watching my uncle compete. Uncle Punkie was a great role model for me, and he impacted my life in ways that words cannot explain.

We moved to Nacogdoches, Texas when I was in the fourth grade and my sister was in the eighth grade. This is the time that my sister really got involved in sports. I had a front-row seat to all her sporting events throughout her high school career. My sister excelled in volleyball, basketball, track, and softball during her high school career. She was the first-ever three-year four-sport athlete in the history of Nacogdoches High School. Side note, the University Interscholastic League s(UIL) did not start softball until her sophomore year. Deidre would practice relentlessly and many times we would compete against each other in the backyard in whatever sport was in season at that time. My sister could have participated in any of her four sports at the collegiate level, but she loved basketball. She earned a scholarship to Sam Houston State University. This meant that I was able to watch her compete for four more years. She was a great college player and I loved getting to watch her play. We would go to games in Huntsville, Houston, and various towns in Louisiana, and of course, we would go to Johnson Coliseum in Nacogdoches to cheer on the Bearkats! I am extremely proud of my sister and thankful for the trail that she blazed. She is another example of what can be accomplished if you focus on the goal and don't let anything distract you.

During my four years of high school, I played football, and basketball and ran cross country and track. Notice I did not say that I excelled at any of those. I did have some success in cross country and track but nothing that would warrant a college scholarship. Eventually, my father and I agreed that I would go to Sam Houston State and attempt to walk on the cross country and track and field teams. We drove to Huntsville to meet Coach Lumley and discuss the possibility of me walking on. I was not sure that he would even agree to let me walk on; however, he did, and I was extremely grateful for the opportunity. This was an open door, and it was time for me to walk. I mean run through it.

From the first day of practice, it was obvious that I was not the same caliber of runner that the other guys on the team were. My teammates would sing songs in jest about how slow I was, and everyone would laugh. They were joking; however, this only steeled my resolve that one day I would do great things. I would imagine myself winning races and being interviewed after the race. Many times, I would sit in front of a mirror and ask myself questions and then answer the questions. So glad nobody ever saw this because I'm sure that I would have looked like a fool. This positive self-talk helped me maintain my focus on my goals and not get discouraged by the daily failures. I did not make a travel squad during the cross country or indoor track and field season so there were many weekends spent in the dorm wondering what it was like to run in college. Finally, the door of opportunity opened at the beginning of the outdoor season. Coach Lumley asked me if I wanted to run the Steeplechase. I did not know what the Steeplechase was, and I did not even think to ask why this was now an option. I immediately said yes, I would like to run the Steeplechase. I later found out that no one else on the team wanted to compete in this event. So, the guy that could not run out of sight in a week if you spotted him two days had his chance to run in college. I learned how to hurdle the barriers as well as navigate a water pit. I did not perfect either of these, by any means. In one of my first races, I did a front flip over the water barrier and looked up to see a spike plate coming at my face as I lay in the water on my back. We then traveled back to Nacogdoches to run at Stephen F. Austin State University (SFA) and I finished last in that race. The icing on the cake was getting lapped in the Steeplechase at the Southland Conference meet. This is not exactly a great start to my collegiate athletic career.

I went back home for the summer. Worked a part-time job that I had during high school, took some classes from SFA and trained as I have never trained before. I did whatever was written on the training calendar and did not think about missing a session. All the failures from the previous year fueled my desire. I would get up early in the morning to run before class and then go to work. Many times, the restaurant I worked at would close around 10:00 PM which meant that I would not get finished until at least 11:00 PM. Therefore, my second run would happen around midnight at Homer Bryce Stadium with the security lights on and I would alternate between running the incline and the flats. Sometimes I would go run at the hottest time of day just to make it more difficult. I did not miss a day all summer because on the wall by my bed was a picture from the race at the conference meet when I got lapped. This was the last thing that I looked at before I went to sleep and the first thing that I looked at when I got up in the morning. My desire to be successful was far greater than wanting to sleep in or take a day off. After a long summer, we began the season with a time trial. The year before I had finished at the back of the pack. Well to the surprise of Coach Lumley and my teammates, I finished in front of everyone.

During the next two years, I competed in cross county, indoor track and field, and outdoor track and field. My performance improved, I made the finals at the conference meet and even scored points for the team. This was a huge improvement over my first year; however, I did not medal, earn all-conference recognition, or ultimately win. Going into my fourth year there was a coaching change. Greg Hinze was coming from Texas A&M and to say everyone was nervous is an understatement. One of my odd jobs was to clean the field house at Bowers Stadium. I would clean the offices at the end of the day and typically the coaches would be in their offices. Coach Hinze was in his office every day and I never introduced myself. We showed up for the time trial at the beginning of the season and in his words "Who would have thought that the janitor would be the best kid on the team!"

During my fourth year, I finished fifth at the conference cross country meet and finished third in the mile at the indoor conference meet. These performances earned me all-conference recognition and I knew that going into the outdoor season the team needed me to score lots of points if we were going to finally get over the hump of finishing second the previous two seasons. It was determined that I would run the 10k, the steeplechase, and the 5k at the conference meet. The conference meet was ironically back in Nacogdoches, and I had a great opportunity to perform in front of my family. Instead of just going out and running, I thought I had to win. I ended up getting lapped out of the 10k by someone that I had beaten earlier in the season. I did not score a point in the 10k and did not help the team at all. The steeplechase was the very next night, and I had a chance to redeem myself. On the very first lap, I hit a barrier and nearly fell. I had to shake that off and go after as many team points as I could get. I ran a personal best in that race which was good enough for second place, eight points for the team, and a new school record. On day three the team race was very close, and I knew that

I had to run well in the 5k for us to win. I ran the best I had ever run in a 5k and finished fourth; one place away from a medal, but only five team points. We ended up in second place again for the third year in a row. Two points out of first place. It does not take a calculator to figure out whose fault it was that we did not win. This weighed on me and still does to this day. I let my teammates down and there was no way around it. Later that summer our Academic Advisor, Cris Thompson wrote me a letter that I still have to this day. In short, she told me that I did my best and that was nothing I could do now to change what happened. Get on to the next thing and focus on doing your best. She has no idea how much this letter meant to me and how her taking a couple of minutes to write a note impacted me for the rest of my life. She was right! There was nothing I could do, and it was time to get back to work.

Going into my senior year, the fifth year, I only had eligibility left in cross country and indoor track and field. Another summer of logging miles, going to school and working part-time jobs just to have an opportunity to win something. This cross country season we had an opportunity to win the team championship. I thought that I had to be the individual champion for us to win. The undue pressure caused me to have several bad races and Coach Hinze decided to send me an e-mail. He told me that no one expects me to do anything except to be tough and run hard. I still have his e-mail. He was right and I just went out and ran hard. That e-mail helped refocus my efforts and I finished third individually and we finished second as a team.

Then it was on to indoor season, and one last go at it. At the conference meet, we decided that I would run the anchor leg of the Distance Medley Relay (DMR), the mile, and the 3k. The indoor conference meet is a two-day meet, on day one I ran the prelims of the mile and qualified for the finals, and then finished the day by anchoring our team to a gold medal and school record in the distance medley relay. At this point, the realization that I only had two more races left was starting to set in. I felt good on day two and the mile was going well. I was in first place until getting out-kicked at the end of the race to finish in second place. One race left and I just wanted to be a champion. I was worn out and tired from three races in less than twenty-four hours getting ready to run the fourth race. The gun went off and during the race, I was in the middle of the pack most of the race. With about four hundred meters to go, I knew that it was now or never. I went for the win with everything that I had and for the first time in my life, I outkicked someone and finished first, and set a school record in the process. After the meet, I was awarded Outstanding Running Athlete of the Year as well as the High Point Athlete.

I look back at someone that started as a walk-on and ended up being the first athlete in Sam Houston history to be the High Point Athlete as well as the Outstanding Running Athlete of the Year. Wow, what a journey! There were many miles logged by myself, yet I was not alone. I saw what my uncle was able to accomplish by being the first person in our family to graduate from college. I had my sister one step in front of me leading the way. My parents always encouraged me. The positive self-talk in the mirror repeatedly played in my mind. I had the letter from Coach Thompson supporting each step I took and the e-mail from Coach Hinze to focus on what I can control. It would have been easy for me to quit my dream, but all the other positive influences would not let me stop believing in my dream.

We have no idea who is watching our journey and how we can positively impact them just by doing our best each day. We don't know the trials someone may be facing in their life. Each day I go to work, and I know that someone is watching. I must be the example for them to follow whether that is another coach or my own children. Words are powerful. Proverbs 18:21 says that death and life are in the power of the tongue. Choose life and speak good things, just like my parents did my entire life or the letter and e-mail I received. Take time to encourage others around you with a quick note or text message. They may be closer than they know to a breakthrough, and you can be the one that lifts them up just a little longer. those things into existence. I firmly believe that no one gets anywhere by themselves, and my life is a testament to how others can positively impact someone's life. Enjoy your daily journey, learn from your failures, get back up and get to work, and don't stop believing!

ABOUT THE AUTHOR:

Social Media:
Email dkoonts1@kleinisd.net
Twitter: @Derek_Koonts

Derek Koonts currently serves as the Assistant Athletic Director for Klein Independent School District. As a lifelong educator, Derek has coached at Sam Houston State University, Texas Christian University, Klein Forest High School, Hightower High School, and Klein High School. During those coaching stents there have been many successes along the way; however, there is nothing better than seeing a former athlete or student and hearing about how well they are doing. After nearly 20 years of coaching, Derek transitioned into administration as an Assistant Principal at Klein Oak High School. At the conclusion of that year, the opportunity of a lifetime presented itself and Derek has been serving student-athletes in Klein ISD ever since. Derek is passionate about supporting coaches and helping them provide the best student-athlete experience for the children we serve. Derek is the proud father of two daughters, Jasmine, and Kathryn, and is married to his best friend, Carol, who is a great role model for their daughters.

ADELBERT TOWNSEND NORWOOD
Derrick L. Pearson

Mentor. Coach. Mentor and Coach.

Mentor. An experienced and trusted adviser. A trainer. Tutor. A trusted counselor or guide. Lead. Pilot. Shepherd. Coach. One who instructs or trains. A trainer. Lead. Pilot. Shepherd. Mentor.

Please allow me to introduce you to the late great Adelbert "Del" Norwood. He was also known as "Red" (did not know that until later in life) but I knew him as Coach. As a team, we would jokingly whisper the name "Delbert" but never loud enough for him to hear us and send us to the hell that is crab walks or wind sprints gift wrapped in baserunning drills. We would announce and crow the word COACH! It was an acknowledgment. It was pride. He was ours. And we were his. COACH!

Coach was tall, athletic, broad, and bright. He had the stride of a thoroughbred. Long strides and strong planting of the foot. Coach could never be small. He did everything TALL. The word that comes to mind now is presence. He was PRESENT. There seemed to be some of his energy around even when he physically was not. There was some of his energy around after he left. When he was physically there, he seemed larger than his already tall frame. His wisdom was like glitter. It remained after the original application. We were better for it.

Our coach was a teacher as well. He taught in the classroom, in the hallway, in the parking lot, on the bus, in the locker room, and on the field. He would teach while coaching other sports, and he would educate you at lunchtime. There was never a time when I crossed paths with Coach that he did not have something new to share with me. He was a walking, talking encyclopedia. He was never off. He shared constantly and consistently. Those words landed with me about Coach, constant and consistent.

He coached at my high school for thirty-two years. I want to pause for a moment and let that land. Thirty-two years. Think of the number of students and athletes he reached. I can try to calculate the number of students and players he impacted. Imagine that kind of influence and add to that the care and love in which he did it. Now consider the families of those students and players, plus their families as well. Coaching through love travels well. It is passed along and shared in different voices, in different families, in different communities, and on different teams. It shows up in the lives of people he never met and will never know. It shows up in victories in sports he did not play or coach, through coaches he never blew the whistle for, and they are all better for it.

Coach. Thirty-two years. Cross Country. Girls Basketball. Baseball. He coached the baseball team to four hundred and twenty wins and nineteen district championships. Two regional titles and one region loss continually haunts me to this very day because he deserved a third and we failed him. His coaching tree was fruitful, with his players becoming heads of baseball programs and teams across this country of ours. The names would take up the entirety of this chapter if I listed them all, but names like Doug Grove, Kevin Clements, Bill Wykoff, Bill Grossman, Mike Murray, Tony Bentley, Horace Willis, Warren Doles, and Rocky Duffy are just some of the names from my time at Washington-Lee (Liberty) High School in Arlington, Virginia. If you reached back or forward any number of years at the school, the numbers impressively increase. He was a proud producer of coaching talent. He was gifted.

I knew of Coach before I got to high school. I had heard stories of his knowledge and experience. He was a former minor league pitcher with stops in San Jose, Roanoke, Charlotte, and Chattanooga among others after studying and playing at the University of Maine. He once told me that he was a better-than-average hitter too. His arm and his bat had not lost a thing some thirty years later. He was still the best pitcher we faced all week, and he could throw this nasty sidearm curveball and fastball, that was often humbling to me and my teammates. We had a lot of success in games played, and he would settle us down and get us back to work by showing us that we did not have the answers to everything. He could also chase his outfielders during practice with some moon shots if we got too close or too comfortable. He never lost it. It was fantastic to watch.

He shared that he loved coaching. Stories told to explain that he gave up the chance to elevate his career to coach. That speaks volumes about the man. He recognized talent, cultivated it, and then set it free in the player. I will say this about the man, he had a great eye for talent and knew how to pull the best from it. He also commanded respect. It was the Marine in him that would show up in his voice from time to time.

I did not play high school baseball as a junior. I was not good enough to make a deep and talented team that year. I decided to play in the county league with friends because it was fun and would keep me out of trouble and in shape for football, which was my first love and my path to college athletics. I had a few successful moments in football as a junior, enough to have some small schools reach out. Baseball was for fun and conditioning. I enjoyed that summer. It also allowed me to reconsider high school baseball the following year. I had seen enough in myself to believe that I could compete and thrive.

I would see Coach in the hallways throughout other sports seasons and he would always stop me and talk. He would mention plays I made in football and basketball, and then suggest how I could get better. He would nudge me into conversations about class and academics. He never once mentioned baseball. Weird. It hit me that he talked about everything except baseball. Some days I thought it was because he thought I was not good enough. Some days I thought it was because I did not think I was good enough. Some days, I thought he was just a nice man. One day, he asked me how good a player who was returning to the team was. I said he was obviously rather good since he made the team the year before. He said he was told by that player that I was better than he was. He mentioned that I played against them in the summer and that I could run. I said that the story was true, laughed, and went to my next class.

After that class, Coach was there in the hallway, waiting. He flashed that million-dollar smile and waved me over. He cornered me to the wall and let out the loudest laugh I ever heard from him. He asked if I knew how fast I was, and I said no. He then waved over the track coach, Jack Walker. Walker barked instead of speaking. He used sounds instead of words. "PEARSON! MMRRRTTNLG" I don't think he ever used words the entire three years I was there. He would grumble, point fingers, and bark orders you may or may not understand. The two men stared at me for an eternity and finally, Walker pointed at Coach and then grumbled something that I deciphered as "are you going to be HIS OR MINE?!!" I pointed at Coach and walked away. (Coach later cornered me again and said that I still should long jump or sprint for Walker when I had extra time. I laughed.)

A recent conversation with a friend reminded me of the fact that I almost did not try out for baseball that year, almost did not make the squad, and almost turned in my uniform one day after a tough day at practice. I tried out the previous year with cracked ribs from football, but that was not why I did not make it. I was not good enough. That stuck in my head. It would be a waste of time. It would not be fun. I should do something else. The day before tryouts, Coach told me the story of facing Willie Mays. Mays had hit a home run against Coach. I was impressed. He was good enough to face him. He quickly added that he had also struck him out. I was impressed.

"What if I had quit before I had the chance?"

I had to give myself the chance. Tryouts were brutal. It was cold. It was windy. I did not have my baseball legs under me. My batting timing was off. I could not show off my throwing arm because we had a talented shortstop with a rifle arm and my job was to simply get the ball to him and let him sniper from short left field. I followed along. I recall making it to the final week of tryouts and was not sure if I would make the team. It was stressful.

My friend also reminded me of my first start, a preseason game against one of our hometown rivals, Yorktown. I was familiar with the guys we would face that day, but I was not sure if or how much I would play. The day before the game, we had some sprints to do for conditioning. Coach yelled out that if you finished first, you did not have to run any more sprints. That was all I needed to hear. I took off and finished first. I smiled for the first time that entire tryout run. I felt like me. I felt good enough. I went home and immediately turned my thoughts to the game.

When I got to the field that Saturday morning, something was different. I was not sure what. As we walked over to the field, I saw the starting lineup. I was in it. I almost lost my breath. We were going to face several pitchers that I had played against in the county league. In my first at-bat, I got a fastball smacked a line drive to deep right-center. I hit the jets and was thinking I would have a double. I peaked at the outfield and saw it got past the centerfielder, so I looked at Coach who was coaching third base. He is waving me to third and this is the part where I ignored Coach as he looked up at me and ran past him at third to score. Coach waited for the dugout celebration to end, grabbed me by the arm, smiled, and said he was sorry for not giving me a signal to stop or go. He yelled that I got there too fast to stop me. He said, "never do that again," but laughed. He then whispered, "What if you had never taken the chance?"

Fast forward to an important regular-season game at Lee and it was the only game that season that I was not in the starting lineup. I was upset. No, I was ANGRY. I remember talking to teammates and I could not let it go. I pouted and whined. Finally, in the late innings,

Coach asked me to pinch-hit in a crucial spot with the tying run on second base. I smashed my helmet over my afro and marched to home plate, not talking to anyone on the way. The first pitch was low and outside but the umpire called it a strike. MORE ANGER. HOW DARE HE! It was the only time that year that I never looked down at Coach in between pitches. I knew the situation. Strike two. It hit me that Coach might want me to bunt for a hit, and even with two strikes, I could get it done. Coach smiled and gave no signal. I hit one to the gap. I put my head down for max speed to get into scoring position at second, but as I round first base, Rocky Duffy was yelling at me instead of giving a signal. "It went out!" I round second in a full sprint, looking for Coach at third so that I did not get in trouble stretching it into a triple and he is there laughing but not giving me a sign for what to do. My teammates are yelling, and Coach says it went out. Having never done it before, I had zero experience in what to do so I kept running hard. It was not until I saw my teammate's cheering did, I slow down, five steps from home plate. More than anything else, I remember Coach laughing. I had never heard him laughing that loud before. That home run won the game, and it is easily my favorite moment of that amazing season because Coach laughed.

I headed back out to left field that inning and he grabbed me by the shoulder. He stared at me and said, "why haven't you been doing that all year?" We laughed together. I said that I was just as surprised as you were, Coach. His laugh is one of my favorite memories.

My friend also recalled another game that included me getting chewed out for stealing home. Our pitcher swung away, and I could have lost some teeth. Coach said that he was worried about if he had my mom's phone number because "I thought you were going to end up in the hospital."

Our last conversation that year was simply Coach finger pointing my chest and demanding that I trust myself, in the game and off the field. He was the first person to call me "talented." He said he would trade his curveball for my speed any day. "Smart and fast is a great pair in life. Please never stop giving yourself the chance." That was followed by the only hug he ever gave me.

Great coaches are great people. Great people make great coaches. The same can be said for teams, families, and communities. But only if we give ourselves a chance.

I really wish I could hear his voice and that accent again.

A coach, their words, and their hug are powerful things.

Miss you today, Coach. Thanking you today, Coach. Loving you today, Coach.

Adelbert Townsend Norwood.
Coach.

ABOUT THE AUTHOR:

Social Media:
IG @derrickpearson
FB @derrick.pearson.5
Email pearsonderrick@aol.com

Derrick Pearson- Sports Radio Station Owner KNTK-FM Lincoln, Nebraska. Co-Host "Old School with Jay Foreman" "DP One on One" at 93.7 The Ticket FM Lincoln, Nebraska. Speaker-TEDxLander May 2019. The love Project Speaker-TEDxDeerPark March 2020. An American Face 3X Amazon Best Selling Author "The Impact of Influence, (Volumes 1&2) Rebuilt Through Recovery

Derrick "DP" Pearson brings his unique brand of energy to The Ticket's programming and direction. DP has spent stops during his career as a sportscaster, radio and television host, writer, manager, and high school coach. That career has taken him nationwide, including Washington, DC, Charlotte, Los Angeles, Salt Lake City, and Atlanta. In addition to his media and coaching ventures, he also helped establish Fat Guy Charities in Charlotte, an NFL Charity, and developed LovePrints, a national mentor program that promotes Loving and Learning through Sports. DP joins Jay Foreman every weekday from 8:00 am – 10:00 am. One on One with DP airs weekdays from 10:00 – 11:00 each weekday morning.

LISTEN AND LEARN
Greg Robinson

One of the first positive and impactful relationships formed, that imprinted on my heart was with my grandfather, William Cortez. You see my mother's family derived from France, Colfax, Iowa, and Junction City, Kansas. My grandfather from Colfax, was in the Army and was last stationed at Fort Riley and retired around Junction City, Kansas. My grandmother, Ginette Cortez, was a seamstress from Verdon, France. They met during the war and were a match made in heaven. They had a son and a daughter and were a great family unit. My mother got married and moved away to Muskogee, Oklahoma with her spouse at a rather early age. As for me and my mom sharing stories over the years, this was a common theme. Her relationship was not positive with her spouse. My mother exited the situation at my birth and we returned to Junction City. My mom did find her true love a few years down the road and married a military Army Tank Engineer named Stanley Robinson, who adopted me and took me under his wing when I was around 8 years old.

So up until then I and my mother resided with my grandparents. Just as you would expect any amazing grandparents to do, they stepped up and helped a single mother raise her child. Mr. Bill Cortez, as he was referred to at work and the Fort Riley golf course, was a person that had a heart of gold. He was a hard worker but wasn't a brute like the tenacious type. Rather, he was easy-going, big-hearted, and very wise. He was one of those that never said much nor raised his voice. When he did speak, he spoke volumes. Little would I know how much my grandfather's hands, wisdom, and love played into the development of a fatherless mixed-race African American boy. Over the next seven to eight years, I and my grandfather grew very close. For as bad as my mother's adversities were, God was blessing her with my and my grandfather's close relationship. During my early developmental years, he doubled as both a grandfather and a father to a kid that wasn't his but was family.

As I'm a dad, an uncle, and a brother now, each unique experience we shared further reinforced the morals and love with which people and situations should be approached with. There's isn't a week that I don't feel and remember Bill's poised spirit and wise impactful moments. I know some situations aren't positive or ideal for young kids. Stepping up and raising a young life that wasn't created by you is done naturally from the heart, as I could imagine occurs frequently within families to this day.

As I got older, I gravitated to sports, being outdoors, and fishing. I had laid roots in Texas. Bill loved to golf and that was his jam. We shared close times when he came to visit. We would frequent local golf courses together. The funny thing is we would never play holes. He always headed to the driving range. It became like meetings of great minds meeting up periodically to discuss where we were in life. My papa would check up on me. We would discuss life, and I would ask questions, like big boy questions. He always had a smooth mindful response. This one time he had a new driver he was testing out. I asked if I could hit with it. He had been crushing the ball seeming to send the ball out the back of the range. I wanted to do that. He had been softly coaching me through the years. I was probably around 16 at this time. He often let out a soft, "Hey son, slow with your backswing, and then you finish hard." He would say, "You're young, you're strong, careful about rushing into things." You will not always be able to go rip-roaring and tearing through things. You'll get it all better when see and feel everything around you first. Educate yourself on what you're doing". He was referring to me keeping my chin down during my swing and keeping my eye on the ball. He was referring to keeping my thumbs aligned on my grip. He was wanting me to not break my left elbow during the backswing. Whew, so many fine points! Hell, I was a 5'9, 265-pound nose guard who benched 465lbs to a top-ranked Texas High school football team. As I set the ball on the tee, I wanted to absolutely crush it! And I couldn't. Well, I could, it was far and few between though. My Papa as I called him would insert himself and model calmly, reissue his instructions on what I needed to pay attention to, and correct. It was his attention to detail and how to apply what you know that taught me first about messages only being as good as they are received. My grandfather, during each occurrence over the years in the driving range, always reminded me to pay attention to myself and be observant of people and things around me. He was so important to me, and our relationship was so strong I trusted everything he said.

A lot of times I hear that resonating voice in my head from my Papa, "slow on the backswing and then you finish hard". I know he is looking down on me and my family almost as if he is still around through events and situations in my life. Those words have helped me apply tons of sense to my life and others. I am a teacher and defensive line coach and daily I get a chance to teach, love, listen, and help young minds practice being observant of themselves, others, and their surroundings, in hopes of helping them make the best decisions possible. Can you imagine being left to approach and navigate this life with minimal or no guidance? Place yourself back in your fourteen- or sixteen-year-old self and some of the trials we all went through. I encounter quite a bit of student-athletes over a day, a week, and years' time, that is down and out and may have a different unique family situation and need that poised calm spirit saying, "slow on your backstroke and then finish hard". As for myself, I'm constantly trying to navigate through this day and age. Always being observant and paying attention to details all around me. Just like that slow on the backswing. I've always kinda had a "don't quit" attitude about adversities. So, I knew how to always finish hard, or simply to have a result of accomplishment or success once finished. Now, I can hit the ball consistently with the driver. I still do not like my papa, but I can hit it. It took some good time over the years. I just needed to give a tad bit of background to help explain how I even got to where Chip Baker and myself are head over heels in love with each other and are all here sharing great experiences.

I was a member of a successful defensive unit and football team in high school. There were coaches and players from all different walks of life. We were diverse, to say the least. Some players came from different socioeconomic backgrounds, as well as different nationalities. Residing around Fort Hood, Texas, the largest active military base in the United States provided that wealth of diversity. One thing we all had in common, as we all sorta chippy competitors but we were a family. We had some amazing coaches that offered a very physically confident brand of football. Each position coach really created strong relationships with players. Coaching-wise, really don't care what sport you coach or at what level, "Players do not care how much you know until they know how much you care." I think that set Killeen - Ellison High apart from other teams during the late 90s. Our head coach Robert Walker brought these players and coaches together as a tuff competitive team. I was able to be a part of a Texas high school football team that was ranked at the top of the State of Texas. So, a winning pedigree was steadily being instilled in me all along. Our coach kept us close. It helped us make very grounded decisions like keeping our grades good and being leaders throughout the school. It impacted us if we let our team or coaches down. Winning and earning a spot on Mike Haney's "swarm" defense was so special, that it meant the world to a sixteen or seventeen-year-old Ellison Eagle football player. While I've heard "winning cures a lot", there is something to be said when one learns and understands the process involved with being successful or winning over and over.

It would be hard to argue that we didn't have one of the best defensive line coaches around in Kenny Washington. I was able to watch and learn from the older players ahead of me. Watching them play and being around Coach Washington was what I set a goal for. Coach Washington had us attacking and reading keys against a down block. We could recognize a puller and get in his hip pocket. We could rush the passer with the signature moves he taught us. He even managed enough film time with us to show us and teach us how to read when screens. This helped me be able to recognize and make a big play for a loss against a tunnel screenplay run by Longview during a playoff game deep in the playoffs. You talk about a great feeling. So many strong powerful impacts in my life thus far.

Fast forward two years. I earned a full ride to Ouachita Baptist University to study and play football. We had a coaching staff turnover after my freshman year. Coach Todd Knight and his new staff took over and with that came lots of changes. Changes that caused coaches to leave and others to come. Also, much tighter reigns, which caused some players to leave also. I knew I had come from a strong background so I told myself I would not be phased by things like this. Rather, stop, remain observant, and keep all the successes I had moving forward. After spring ball concluded with the new staff, I sat with Coach Derby my college defensive line coach. In college, before you prepare for the summer, you have exit meetings where coaches lay out their expectations of the summer and want to hear the goals and aspirations we have for the following season. Coach Derby was absolutely a high motorcoach. He was one of the most intense coaches I'd been coached by. He was incredibly funny and very business-like and very detailed with his expectations. Like, he was able to flip a switch and go from on the field Derby to college professor/mentor/coach Derby. Shoot, when I say we had meetings, we had meetings every day! Sometimes multiple meetings a day.

Coach Derby was very time-oriented. You were not late to meetings, weights, film, or anything associated with the defensive line. The time had come for our exit meeting. Our very first one. My first one. The meeting went as expected. We reviewed my grades, team member qualities, production, expectations for the summer, and goals for next year. We got the production part and that is where things took a turn. This man flat out looked me into my eyes and told me he was going to try his best to out recruit me. I asked what does this mean? Are you getting rid of me? He told me he has offered three defensive tackles. He hopes that they will all be better players than me. You will either accept it and get outplayed or you will continue to work and become even better. Ok, so I was not an "all-conference" player. I was a strong, quick coachable player. I'd like to think I wasn't bad. I was just doing it all out of a 5'9 now 285lb body. I can say that just flat-out colligate football was simply tougher than anything I had experienced in high school. I had gone up against big, fast, and even the nastiest of offensive linemen and had successes.

So, I couldn't figure out why this guy is attacking me and my play. He told me he didn't care that I had broken the bench press record as a freshman or that I even played and started as a freshman. Simply put he replied, "You get out of something what you put into it. I need more. I need more production. I need more leadership." he sternly put it. He then went on to tell me "Teddy, you have experienced some successes early. What is going to drive you from here on out?" He told me that his job was to get the best out of me. He then again took another jab in telling me he didn't care where I was from or how good my high school football experience was, we are in the now. Coach Derby told me he was going to try to find a guy that was stronger than me, that was taller than me, and a guy that could outplay me! He mentioned that I had failed three of my pre-summer conditions times. Meaning, that I failed to make three of the eighteen one-hundred yard gassers! He also did his research and informed me before I got too "big in the britches", that I had slacked in one of my classes and went from an A to a D. I wasn't crushed, but rather humbled by what had transpired. Okay, I did get my feelings hurt a tad. Man, I was breathing heavy and sweating as though I was ready to go play. I was offended so badly. He pretty much-established accountability with me. I'm pretty sure he knew I could handle it but also knew I had a little chip on my shoulder. He was sure to try to knock it off, but I would rise to the challenge. With where I had come from, I was not going to back down from any high expectations. Rather, I made a pact within myself, to take care of business and prove naysayers wrong.

Leaving that meeting, I went into such a reflection period. It was fueled by not wanting to let my coach down or get replaced. There was a huge growth that occurred within me. You know how there's the saying that "if you have to ask, you probably already know the answer?" Well from that day forward, "you get out of something that you put into it" is on replay with a lot of what I do. Often that statement alone helped me distinguish between right and wrong or maybe what morally may be the most sensible plan of action. When you take a look or have a conversation with someone who is successful, driven, recovering, or struggling, what have they put in? Why are they getting what they are getting out of it? As you can see, relationships and sports were influential in my life. Some of the hardest, toughest lessons I have learned and may not have understood then, hit ten times harder now that I am a husband, father, brother, coach, friend, and mentor. I can't help but take these experiences with me and apply or share what I've experienced. I've been taught never to hold on to "it" but to pass "it" along. I am truly thankful for my wife Candice and my family that has always been supportive and loving to help keep Coach Robinson alive and kicking.

ABOUT THE AUTHOR:

Social Media:
IG @coachcatfish
FB @coachcatfish
Email str8texn@hotmail.com

Hello to all. Thank you for taking the time to read my chapter. My name is Greg Robinson. Two things I love in my spare time are fishing and cooking real cook food. I am a proud husband to my amazing wife Candice. We have been married fifteen years and have known each other all of our life. She is my best fishing buddy. We have two children together. My daughter Angelina who is seven years old going on seventeen. We have a son Isaiah, who is eighteen years old and will go down as one of the goats! Lots of great stories behind him. Isaiah is a great guy and a budding young man with his head on straight and full of charisma.

I have been a teacher and a football coach with many subjects and sports under my educator umbrella. Through the years of education, my stops have included: Arkansas Tech University, Killeen Alternative School Campus, Nolan Junior High, Ellison High, San Antonio East Central, Conroe High, and Caney Creek High School. I have been educating and coaching for twenty-three years now. I have taught a range of subjects from speech, health, and PE, adaptive PE, and outdoor education to Teen Leadership. I would easily say that teaching life and how to be functional and thrive in relationships has been most rewarding while teaching Teen Leadership.

Thus far the most fun name calling for me is "Ol' Ball Coach"! I have coached soccer for both men's and women's divisions. I have been a head coach for each also. I have coached the discus and shot put for women and men in track. I have also been the head coach as well.

I've had the most fun opportunities and relish in coaching defensive line play. I've played with absolute studs! I've been coached by greats in my eyes. Gosh, I still love the process and preparation that goes into the game. I've been cut from an old school cloth so to speak. An era where a good handshake, eye contact, and yes sir no ma'am is genuinely the standard. An era where we drank from a PVC pipe with holes for spouts hooked to a hose for water breaks. I played football and soccer all my life. As my mom would tell me, "You need to take your big behind back outside and play some more instead of eating all my groceries up!" So, I have always been around sports and the outdoors.

I graduated from Ellison High in Killeen Texas in 1998. I attended Ouachita Baptist University and studied kinesiology and minored in Speech Communications. I was fortunate and blessed to play on an incredibly successful high school football team. I totally have coaches, teammates, and our school culture to thank for that. Texas High School football is the front doorway to High school. In the fall everyone loves little Friday night lights. Furthermore, I was able to earn a full Football scholarship at Ouachita where I played for four years and graduated in 2002. Coming from a family where I was the first college graduate was a huge accomplishment.

So much of life transpires with our experiences. At times I had a little knucklehead in me or what my dad called "being hardheaded". It is with thanks to the many members of my villages who helped have a part in my growth. If it weren't for a few people, there definitely could have been some negative outcomes. The teachable moments in life are probably what drive me the most in my daily quest to inspire, coach, and encourage. I love teenagers because they are free-spirited and full of energy and haven't had the life sucked out of them too badly, unlike some adults. They are very impressionable. Just look at what trends! So much of who I am is built on relationships. I am a huge relationship-building guy! My close relationships with others allowed trust to become evident. Once trust is established, records and barriers will be broken or built up. You will read shared moments of breakthrough experiences that helped me succeed.

HOW DO YOU BECOME CONFIDENT?
Hoss Tabrizi

One second left on the clock. The home crowd erupts. Down by one. The ball is in your hands. The other team calls for a timeout to "ice" you.

What's going on in your mind at this moment? What are you thinking about? Missing? Disappointing your team? A previous play that should have put you in the lead? Or are you thinking about how many times you've made this play in practice? Are you thinking about how you are the best person on your team, on this court, on this field, on this planet, and that you can win this?

What are you thinking about?

If you think negatively, fear and doubt creep in. When this happens, there is very little chance you win. You'll tense up. Your muscles will hold you back. You'll limit oxygen to your lungs. These things will reduce your odds of success.

If you think positively, your confidence will put you in the best mind frame to perform. You'll be loose. Your muscles will relax. You'll win.

A coach's job is to empower athletes with confidence. This responsibility applies to all leaders; parents, teachers, managers, and mentors must create a culture of confidence. We need the confidence to beat the defender one on one, execute plays, do our jobs, learn from our mistakes, and move on from the past.

In this chapter, you'll learn what creates confidence and what gets in the way. You'll hear from various coaches and athletes about why they are confident and what they do to create that culture for those around them.

Confidence is having the ability to be proud of the greatness around you and elevating those around you. It doesn't involve jealousy or hate; it is believing in yourself and your teammates. Confidence can be quiet or loud depending on one's personality. Sometimes it can be mistaken for arrogance.

Confidence to me means trusting oneself to perform regardless of the situation. The keyword there is trust. Confident teams trust the process and the system. Confident teams trust that setbacks are temporary. They don't play as just five players on a basketball court. When they attack, the opponent feels like they are playing against seven or eight players, not five. Confident football and soccer teams look like they have fourteen or fifteen players on the field. Why is that? Confidence makes them quicker, more accurate, stronger, and smarter.

If you don't believe me, think of the opposite mindset. What happens when you're riddled with fear and doubt? You second-guess what you should do instead of just playing and reacting, which makes you slower, and being slow generally leads to mistakes and failure. A fifteen-point deficit becomes a thirty-point deficit. Confidence, on the other hand, reminds you that you can reduce this fifteen-point deficit to ten, then to six, until, all of a sudden, fear and doubt are in the other team's mind.

I've coached athletes from age three to twenty-two. Lately, I've been coaching kids at a young age because I'm involved in youth sports with my own kids. What's great about coaching youth sports is the responsibility that comes with it. On top of developing players, coaches have to make the game fun while also teaching life lessons along the way. In this way, coaches can serve as parental figures or role models.

I coached youth basketball in the winter of 2021-2022. Most kids between the ages of three and ten are novices at their sport. At the beginning of the season, a couple of parents had to drag their five and six-year-old daughters to the gym to go to practice. One of the moms told me that, a few months ago, her daughter wouldn't get out of the car for the whole season of soccer because was anxious and afraid of failure.

Working with kids as a competitive person, I had to redefine what winning meant to me. The objective was no longer to score more points than the opponent; it was to make practice fun and to elevate everyone's skill level enough so that they'd keep playing the sport. I redefined winning as empowering each kid with confidence so they could enjoy the sport of basketball as much as I did as a kid. By the end of the season, kids that couldn't even hit the net with the ball during the first practice made multiple baskets in a row and had swagger while doing it. #Winning.

Many people lack confidence, but it is something that can be developed over time. Here are some tips to become more confident:

1. Create Challenges

"He who is not courageous enough to take risks will accomplish nothing in life."
Muhammad Ali.

I've coached different levels of teams. When I was an AAU basketball coach, I traveled across the country and coached against various teams in basketball tournaments. Travel sports create a different, and often greater, challenge for athletes. If you are the best player on your team, how good are you? What if you are the best player in your neighborhood? What if you are the best player in your district or city? How do you measure the challenge?

Competing against kids in other cities and states allows you to face new challenges. Without worthy competition, false confidence is created. Real confidence comes from overcoming failure, having grit, being resilient, and succeeding after dealing with challenges.

When I asked a former two-sport athlete and current successful attorney, Jachele Velez, how she's confident, she told me, "I've been able to throw since before I could walk. I was raised in a baseball family. By the time I started little league, I was better than the boys, so that gave me a lot of confidence."

Jachele credited her parents for the role they played in creating a culture of confidence. Her parents were her primary coaches until high school, and they provided her with a balance of support and constructive criticism. Since I coach young girls and am a "#girldad" myself, I had to know more about what cultivated all this for Jachele. "I was constantly in front of people as a child," she told me. "You name it—church plays, speaking competitions, school plays, etc.—I was at ease in ways others probably weren't at an early age."

In other words, from an early age, she was constantly facing new challenges.

I want to thank my mother, Nahid, and my father, Mehdi, for creating a culture of confidence for me as I was growing up and for teaching me the importance of making my kids Maximus, Mia, and Michael confident.

Challenge your kids. From a young age, teach them how to swim, ride a bike, or do chores around the house. As parents and coaches, we must challenge our kids and athletes. The sense of resilience that comes from failure and the lessons and joy that come from accomplishing difficult tasks will have a profound impact on your child's confidence.

2. Preparation

"Confidence for me comes from being 100% sure that you know exactly what to do in a given situation. So, confidence is not an externally given thing but rather an internally produced feeling born of discipline and preparation. Discipline is doing the right

thing, at the right time, every single time. So, confidence is tied to discipline."
Legendary basketball coach, Fred Priester.

Confidence is feeling comfortable with something that makes others uncomfortable because you've experienced it so many times already. In sports, you hear the saying that ninety percent of the game is mental. There's a reason why elite teams and players practice until perfection is achieved. The repetition of game-like events at game-like speed in practice prepares players by giving them the instinct to know what to do if something similar happens in a game. Kobe Bryant would practice his fadeaway jump shot five hundred times a day. Seeing and hearing the ball go through the net that many times gave him the confidence that won five NBA championships

I asked the two most prestigious and successful coaches that I have had the pleasure of knowing where confidence comes from, and they both said preparation.

Fred Priester is a couple of games shy of eight hundred wins as a high school basketball coach. He said, "Doing the right thing isn't hard. Knowing the right thing to do is hard and that is where preparation comes into play. A coach who fully prepares his team and then requires the accountability needed to develop discipline is building true confidence. Confidence is built by preparation and discipline, and it holds up when things get tough. Confident teams are successful because they have a firm foundation of preparation, both physically and mentally. They are trained by the discipline of accountability. Hebrews 12 says, "No discipline seems pleasant at the time, but painful. Later on, however, it produces a harvest of righteousness and peace for those who have been trained by it" (Hebrews 12:11 [NIV]). Great confidence has its roots in discipline.

I have experience coaching with Coach Priester, so I have seen how his teams master offenses and set plays and how this preparation gives them the confidence to score regardless of their opponents' actions.

When I asked Washington Metropolitan Basketball Hall of Fame Coach Red Jenkins where confidence comes from, he stated, "You'll play confidently when you put in the work and are prepared. If you've paid the price, then you'll be ready. That price is hard work and preparation. Hard work makes you very confident."

I asked Coach Jenkins to give an example of his team's confidence, and he told me, "If we showed a move to Tommy Amaker (former Duke basketball player and current head coach at Harvard University) in practice, he would go to the James Lee Center and work on it. He would work on it so much that he would come back to practice the next day with it perfected! Preparation is key!"

Because Tommy would have practiced the move until he could only do it right, he would have the confidence to use it in a game.

Former professional athlete and current US Army Green Beret, Joe Oliver talked about preparation as well. He said, "My confidence comes from prior preparation, a mental minimization of the impact of failure, and past success, in that same order of importance."

Short and to the point. Joe Oliver speaks to preparation and the right mindset as well.

3. The Right Mindset

"I've missed more than 9,000 shots in my career. I've lost almost 300 games. 26 times I've been trusted to take the game-winning shot and missed. I've failed over and over and over again in my life. And that is why I succeed."
Six-time NBA champion, Michael Jordan.

I asked my six-year-old daughter, Mia Tabrizi, why she's so confident, and she told me, "If I mess up, it doesn't mean I'm not good at it. People make mistakes even when they are really good at something because nobody is perfect."

It sounds like both the six-year-old and the six-time champ are on to something.

As a competitive person, winning matters to me, but wins and losses both matter when developing a player. Losses should be used as a tool to get better, not to beat oneself up. Wins are something to celebrate, but the scoreboard can also cloud what's important when it comes to youth sports, which is learning and having fun. Instead of saying, "You are going to score five goals today!" to a developing player, encouraging fun and achievable goals will build confidence.

Resilience is a learned skill that teaches you failures are temporary. About twenty years ago, there was a Converse shoe commercial with Dwayne Wade that showed him getting knocked to the ground seven times. Then, the video ends with, "Fall down seven times. Get up eight."

Perseverance is a word that has stuck with me for more than twenty-five years. To me, it is the ability to commit to something that's difficult without giving up. As a kid, I would often hear the quote from NC State Basketball Coach, Jimmy Valvano, on ESPN, "Don't give up. Don't ever give up." That always stuck with me. I don't give up and, because of that, I know I can overcome most things.

The right mindset empowers you to take on any challenge or obstacle. Persevere, and you'll be confident.

4. Determination

"There may be people who are more talented than you, but there is no excuse for anyone to work harder than you."
Hall of Famer, Derek Jeter.

One of the greatest coaches of all time, Vince Lombardi, once said: "The price of success is hard work, dedication to the job at hand, and the determination that, win or lose, we have applied our best to the task at hand."

Kobe's ritual of shooting five hundred shots a day shows determination. The beautiful thing about becoming a great shooter is that it can be done with the proper work ethic and determination. The majority of NBA players weren't great shooters when they got there. Determination accomplishes more than talent alone.

People with determination and a strong work ethic naturally have confidence, which puts them one step ahead of those who don't. When you dedicate yourself to your craft for long enough, fear and anxiety wash away. With the proper amount of time dedicated to a skill, competence increases, which leads to confidence. You just have to stay determined and keep practicing until you get it right.

I had a friend that I used to play tennis with. He was pretty good at tennis since he played in high school, and I picked up tennis in my thirties. Naturally, he would beat me every time we played. At one point, he had beat me in forty-nine matches without me winning a single one. Yes, I counted.

It didn't bother me that I lost to him because I knew I'd eventually win. I had the confidence that I would beat him someday, and I was determined to keep improving until I won. It took thousands of hours of training and practice, but I finally did beat him. Before he won his fiftieth match against me, I beat him three times. He never played me again after that.

Determination leads to success. Success leads to confidence.

The lessons that we learn as athletes stay with us for life and can be applied to any challenges that we may face. Some of the best employees in the workforce are former athletes. They've challenged themselves, prepared, persevered, and stayed determined, so they have the confidence to get the job done.

Confidence is contagious and has a snowball effect. It's thrilling to see the ball go through the net a couple of times in a row, and this confidence builds up the momentum to make several more shots. But confidence also allows you to miss eight shots in a row and still shoot because you know the next one is going in.

Confidence doesn't exist magically; you have to learn it. Anyone can become confident. If you lack confidence, work harder, and stay determined. Change your mindset, and see failure as a teacher, not as a loss.

If you are not confident, prepare until you are. If you are confident, make sure you challenge yourself so that the confidence is battle-tested and genuine.

ABOUT THE AUTHOR:

Social Media:
IG @hoss.tabrizi
FB @hoss.tabrizi
Email hoss.tabrizi@nm.com

Hoss Tabrizi is the son of Mehdi and Nahid and brother to Nahaleh. He's married to Carolyn, and together they have three children: Maximus, Mia, and Michael. He's a financial advisor, coach, bestselling author, public speaker, and community leader.

Hoss genuinely wants to help people become better and to discover their inner greatness. He cares about seeing improvement in himself and in those that he interacts with. Hoss communicates with people in a way that motivates them to have confidence and conviction on their journey towards self-improvement in their personal, professional, and financial lives. Just like his father, he wants to leave this world better than he found it.

INSPIRED TO COACH
Jason Haddock

"Every coach had a coach that inspired them to be a coach."

This saying has popped up on my social media accounts no less than a dozen times in the last week. Every time I see it, I smile and keep scrolling. It's a nice sentiment, meant to give some meaning to what we do as coaches. I must admit that it is absolutely true. When I think about why I followed the call to coach, and, make no mistake, coaching is a true calling, I find myself reminiscing on the examples that my own former coaches set for me. So, I must agree with that saying; I had coaches that inspired me to become a coach.

As seasons start to wrap up for the school year, I feel the need to reflect on how our teams performed. I sit back and look at the data: wins and losses, weights that went up or down, times that decreased as athletes got faster, and accolades they garnered in the post-season. Analytics is easy to look at, but the internal development of our athletes is harder to measure. Despite this, I would argue that this kind of growth is far more important than how many tackles they had in a game or how far they threw the discus.

For most of our athletes, high school is the farthest they'll go in their sport. For those fortunate enough to play at the next level, college will likely be their last hurrah. For the very few, the elite, a pro-career will be their future, but this is not the case for everyone.

After graduation, most high school athletes will enter the world of normalcy: working a nine-to-five, paying bills, and starting families. For the vast majority of our athletes, their sports accomplishments will be a fleeting memory from their youth, but the lessons that coaches teach them will last a lifetime.

So, after twelve years of coaching, I have to ask myself, what impact did I have on my athletes this year? Sometimes we see the results immediately, but often we don't see them for years.

Before I look at my athletes, I have to look at myself and ask who had an impact on me. Sure, I had great coaches in high school and college. I had a memorable football career and teammates who are lifelong friends. But did I have a coach who really made an impact on my life, who mentored me as an athlete *and* as a person? Thankfully, I did. I can easily point out one coach who inspired me to become a coach myself and to give back to my athletes.

In 1995, my family moved to Marble Falls, Texas. I was a sophomore who was ready to get to work with my new team. Also new that year was Coach Donny Funderburg. He was only a few years older than me and in his second year of teaching and coaching. Perhaps that was my initial draw to want to play for him. He got along easily with the guys on the team. He was funny and joked around but still commanded respect from us. Funderburg coached offense, and even though I was a defensive player, he helped all of his athletes, no matter our position.

Coach Funderburg was a coach you wanted to please; you wanted to make him proud with the results of your hard work. For a job well done, getting a pat on the back and a "great job" from him was more than rewarding. When things didn't quite go our way, he'd still put his arm around us and tell us he loved us and appreciated our effort.

He knew we played our hearts out, and we respected him. In my senior year, I once jokingly called him "Donny" while getting on the bus. I'll never forget the look he gave me; it was a look that said, "Child, have you lost your mind?" I knew he wasn't mad at me, but I also knew he was serious. To this day, twenty-four years later, I still rarely use his first name.

As the youngest coach on the staff, Coach Funderburg became the adopted coach by my mom, one of the team's boosters. Every Sunday during the season when the booster moms brought food up to the coaches while they prepared for the upcoming week, she made sure to bring him his own buttermilk pie. Each week, it became sort of a joke if Coach Funderburg would get his pie or not.

Over time, he became part of the family. I was able to spend more time around him and see how he did the things he did. I learned a tremendous amount by watching his interactions with my peers. I saw how he treated the athletes with respect and how it differed from the typical old-school, a hard-nosed approach that most coaches used. Though the things he coached us on were no different from what the old hats did, the way he did it was.

After football was over my senior year, I played soccer simply because Coach Funderburg was the head soccer coach. I wanted to have a little more time together before I graduated. Playing soccer for him led me to try out for (and make) the club soccer team during my freshman year in college. His influence also led to my first job in education where I coached both football and soccer. The simple act of playing a sport for a coach in high school directly impacted my first job in education and coaching.

Coach Funderburg often gave guys rides home after practice or games if they needed it. Seeing several players in his truck wasn't uncommon. Oftentimes, he would even buy them food on the way home. He took care of those athletes that needed a little extra, and it meant the world to him. I distinctly remember once that he bought cleats for one of our "football-to-soccer converts" that didn't have the right ones or the money to get them. I can only imagine that the look of shock on that kid's face filled Coach Funderburg with happiness. He didn't do it for recognition or gratitude. He did what he did because that's just who he is.

After my first year in college playing soccer, I "walked on" to the football team, going back to the game I truly loved. Coach Funderburg also moved to a different high school and was coaching less than an hour away from where I was. Their staff came out to watch practice once. I remember thinking that I had another chance in practice to make him proud of the player I was. That day was one of my more memorable practices.

Years of playing for Coach Funderburg and watching him help others have influenced who I am as a coach. I hold my athletes to a high standard, but I'm compelled to hold myself to a high standard as well. I still ask myself, "What would Coach think?" when I'm running a drill or preparing the weekly game plan. I have grown to adopt his model of "coach them hard, but love them hard". I take care of some of my athletes the same way he did. I do my best to let my athletes know that what occurs on the field is business, but that, off the field, I can put my arm around them, love on them, and mentor them.

I do my best to make sure my athletes are taken care of by checking on them academically. I know I also have to check on them mentally and emotionally as well. Much of the professional development I do is related to player development as well. I'm constantly thinking about how I can develop my athletes into better young adults.

My athletes know that once they're mine, they're always mine. I'm there for them even after graduation. Several of my former players are still close with me, and I have continued to grow those relationships. Often, they come asking for advice. Likewise, I still ask Coach Funderburg for advice. In 2018 while coaching at Marshall High School, we had a player murdered the week of the state semifinal game. My first call after getting the news was to Coach Funderburg to ask advice on how I could best take care of my players as we traveled that path together.

I still try to do things that would make Coach Funderburg proud of me. Recently, I spoke with him about a job interview I had for a head football coach position. We discussed the interviewing process, and he told me that he was proud of me and always had been.

Donny Funderburg had a major impact on me as a high school athlete. That impact helped shape my future as an educator and coach. I strive to do the same as I educate, coach, and mentor my current student-athletes. Coach Funderburg was the best man at my wedding. We have remained close; even decades after he last coached me, he continues to impact my life. Ultimately, I pray that I can continue to influence others the way he influenced me.

ABOUT THE AUTHOR:

Social Media:
Email jason.a.haddock1@gmail.com

Jason Haddock is a native of Marble Falls, Texas. He earned a Bachelor's degree in Applied Mathematics from Baylor University, where he spent three years playing linebacker for the Bears. He also earned a Master's degree in Kinesiology and Sports Management from TWU.

Coach Haddock has coached for over twelve years during which time he's worked with several future collegiate athletes in football and track. He has been part of several Texas programs that have won state titles. He has been published twice in AFCA magazine and has spoken at Glazier, AFCA, and other clinics, where he discussed football, growth in athletic programs, and culture change.

Coach Haddock continues to teach and coach high school football in Texas. He and his wife, Jamie, are parents to Adalina and Isabella Haddock.

THE SUPERSIZING LOT OF INFINITE POSSIBILITIES
Jessica Perez

Infinite possibilities do exist. They exist when we amplify our thoughts, actions, and beliefs to impact and influence growth along our ever-evolving journeys. Therefore, let me take you into the mind of this author who has spent so much of the past few decades coaching others to become their best selves by diving into the philosophy of...supersizing their lot. Take the leap and see how redefining your lot is the key to unlocking the infinite possibilities that lie ahead.

Supersize is a word that has stuck in society as the way to upgrade your fast-food order and get that quick fix. But to me, the word has an entirely different meaning. To me, supersizing isn't about fries or soda; it is about growing exponentially.

Lot is a word that has several meanings. It can refer to an area of property with clearly defined borders. Envision a rectangular plot of land with boundary lines that mark who owns which lot. Can you imagine it? To me, defining your own lot in life is an opportunity where infinite possibilities exist.

These two philosophies that I have embraced throughout my life have led me to be a contributing author for this book. I am so excited to have you begin your own Supersizing Journey that will help you break free from your own lot.

Let me take you through a short (no pun intended) example of true growth. Standing at four-foot-eleven, I defied the odds in sports. I also pushed the limits when it came to my career aspirations; I wanted to be a sportscaster in a time when little girls didn't do that. With the odds against me, I was inspired by an amazing village of influencers who encouraged me to step outside of the lot that was supposed to be my destiny. Supersizing became the pivot I needed to truly grow.

I graduated in the top five percent of my predominately male Sports Administration program while also being a two-sport athlete in sports that I had never played competitively before college. That's right, this spunky four-foot-eleven woman proved that size doesn't really matter.

Following college, I became an educator, athletic director, high school/travel coach, co-founder of a charter school and non-profit, city manager, executive director, network marketer, and inspirational keynote speaker. And the list continues to grow.

So, the big question is, how did I accomplish all that? Not once, but consistently along my journey, I simply applied a supersizing philosophy to overcome the boundaries of my lot.

We all are born into a lot. Yes, an actual lot inside our own minds: a limiting, oppressive, traditional blueprint that is created by our environment and our circle of influence. If we believe it to be our safest and most direct route to success, we almost always choose to stay inside of that pre-disposed lot and never venture past the boundary lines.

Defining L.O.T.

Limiting

Imagine a little girl by the name of Jessica, saying, "I want to be a professional athlete," to her private Catholic school teacher in 1973. She was told to pick another career. Then, when that same little girl said, "I want to be a sports broadcaster," she was told that this was the wrong answer once again. The teacher sent her home to talk with her mom and come back with a career that was a better fit for her. She did, and her answer was this, "My mom says I can be whatever I want so, I want to be a professional athlete who is also a sports broadcaster." From that day on, little Jessica became the reader at every function the school or church had and played on the middle-school teams as a fourth-grader. Supersizing conversations like this one still impact how I coach athletes, business leaders, and colleagues today.

Oppressive

Staying within our limitations holds us back and inflicts hardship. The lot that we are given in life often prevents us from accomplishing growth and greatness. We often don't think that we can move past the boundaries inside our minds. It is like that story of a young child playing in their front yard with a parent who never wants them to go past the fence line for fear of injury. While we all understand the importance of safety, we also should realize the power of stepping past that "fence" and seeing what the world has to offer outside of those boundary lines. Our mindsets can become oppressive if we never allow ourselves the opportunity to leap past our comfort zones.

Traditional

A lot is something that is done habitually as a part of a tradition that is long-established. This is a mindset I embrace but also one that I continue to challenge. There are some amazing traditions within my Hispanic upbringing including celebrations, family, food, music, and so much more. Women in sports, though, was a challenging concept to the traditionalists, as well as little girls who liked to climb trees and be outdoors. Breaking the barriers while grabbing hold of mentors who valued uniqueness and out-of-the-box thinkers was exactly the mindset I needed to break from tradition and truly become a super sizer in life. This is where the lot began to crumble, and the possibilities began to gain traction. In these micro-moments, a supersized path was born, filled with the belief needed to evolve, shift, pivot, and lean into the next phase of progress.

The first step to breaking out of your lot is to think bigger, like really big, the biggest you ever have. It is all about expanding your mindset. Ask yourself these powerful questions:

1. Who are you? What drives you? What are you most excited about? Where have you come from? What makes you, you?
2. What is your goal in life? Have you ever really thought about that?
3. What do you want to contribute to humanity?

You see, the answers to these questions will drive your message, your reason for being, and your path to the call to action you have been seeking. So...get to work! Ask yourself these questions, put the answers down on paper, and get ready for the second tool that will forge the way to the shift.

The second step to breaking out of your lot is to do bigger, like super-duper big! Take the leap, rip off the band-aid, and simply take the action that you have talked about, dreamt about, but never acted on. For me, that step two was a big deal. At times, it seemed daunting, but at the moment, the leap was liberating. I had enough fear to keep me humble and enough confidence to ground me as it was happening.

The third step to breaking out of your lot is to become bigger, that is, in my words "to supersize on the daily". This means taking your lot and elevating it. That's right, elevate, influence, and impact so that all facets of you are supersized; your voice, mind, and heart will absolutely be heard. In every moment you live, every relationship you build, every career path you take, and every connection you make, supersize the moment. Become bigger than you have ever been. See, I walk into a room, not as a four-foot-eleven woman but as a six-foot-eleven catalyst for impact.

Choices are possible, connections matter, and becoming a catalyst for change is well within our journeys. Infinite possibilities are within our reach when we supersize the lots we live in, and we answer those defining questions. Once we build the beliefs of thinking bigger, doing bigger, and becoming bigger, the growth we desire will happen.

I hope you will put supersizing into action as soon as you finish reading this chapter. Go on. Take that pen, and begin your steps to becoming a supersizing, lot-breaking, catalyst-creating, leader of your own destiny.

ABOUT THE AUTHOR:

Social Media:
IG @jessica_jlo_perez
FB @JessicaJLoPerez
Email perezjess141@gmail.com

Jessica Perez is a fourth-generation native to Tampa, FL who still lives, serves, and influences there. She grew up in a family-centered community that instilled the values of connection, relationships, loyalty, and impact. Jessica is a product of that "you can do anything" mindset, and she began a leaping journey to take on massive challenges in academics and athletics while growing through them.

Jessica graduated from St. Thomas University as a two-sport collegiate athlete and began her career in education as a physical educator, athletic director, and coach in private, public, and charter schools for eleven years. She co-founded Trinity School for Children in Tampa. She also dove into the non-profit world as a co-founder of CANDO Sports, Inc. over twenty-five years ago and still serves on their board. From education to local government, Jessica began a career with the City of Tampa as a Parks and Recreation professional. Her tenure included serving as manager for over two hundred employees, overseeing parks, a marina, community centers, pools, and art studios.

After a great career in both education and parks and recreation, Jessica dove into the world of entrepreneurism and network marketing. She has become a leader in her publicly traded wellness company named LifeVantage (LFVN) and is actively pursuing to speak, educate, and lead the charge in pioneering nutrigenomics while growing a leveraged global business. In addition, she is a certified trainer with the Positive Coaching Alliance and has delivered over four hundred workshops on the topics of leadership, coaching, and character development. She is much sought after as a coach, consultant, and catalyst for change.

A DAUGHTER'S TALE
Maggi Welham

The coach, leader, mentor, and friend that had the most profound impact on my softball career was my father. Many athletes have the same relationship with a family member whose encouragement, guidance, pressure, insane badgering, and constant fussing have lifted them to the person they are today and the person they will become in the future. But my father seemed to be on a whole other level. He pushed me hard and was a tough love kind of man.

Even though he was my biggest fan, my father made sure I was prepared for the outside world that he knew would hit me and hit me hard. His way to get me ready for the ultimate contest of life was through this magnificent game of softball. This little yellow ball-shaped so much of my journey. I cannot even explain it. It is amazing to think how a twelve-inch ball, a seventeen-inch long plate, a forty-three feet pitching mound, a two-hundred-foot fence, and sixty feet of stolen freedom can change your life.

My dad taught me how to use every inch to my advantage, probably due to my small stature. He was the person who hit me ball after ball, caught my two hundred pitches nearly every single day, built a concrete structure for me to throw to when no one was available and replaced our backyard fence when I completely knocked it down.

My dad decided I was not ready to go off to college and would stay in town and play softball and so that is what I did. In those two years, I played third base, shortstop, and second base at Incarnate Word College. I accumulated many accolades from All-Conference to an All-American nomination and held a few records for my dad to be proud of and to recapture his absolute love for me and the game. But I still knew I had much bigger places to be than the ones chosen for me.

You see my dad was by far my favorite person on earth and his approval and pride meant more to me than anything, but I had to leave. I had this deep yearning to play Division I softball and regardless of who was in my way, even my biggest admirer, I knew I had to go.

I began developing my plan, my getaway. I was researching colleges and looking at where I wanted to play when discovered the University of Tennessee at Chattanooga. The coaches at this university were the current Olympic coaches, so I knew I had to get there and be a part of this. I know a pretty lofty goal for a five-foot-two, one hundred pound kid from San Antonio who wasn't even asked to be there. But to me at the ripe old age of nineteen, it made absolutely perfect sense, and from that moment I was not taking no for an answer, I was about to put the wheels in motion.

I started with my parents, explaining to them I was ready for a change. I am unsure if they believed me right away or if they just felt compelled to be supportive in any way imaginable, but they were. I am the youngest of four, from a very tight-knit Hispanic family. Both my sisters played softball at Incarnate Word and graduated from there. My brother's move to College Station to attend Texas A&M was a huge family ordeal, so my leap as the baby of the family to Tennessee was unbearable for my folks.

I felt that I had their support in my dream, so I called the coach and introduced myself, and explained I had applied and would be accepted to the university. I told him I was coming to school and would love an opportunity to try out. He asked me a lot of questions and we discussed my previous accolades and accomplishments. I mailed him all my college statistics and quite possibly a VHS tape. He explained how he had no money for me; I could try out, and if I made it I could walk on.

I was leaving a full-tuition scholarship, room and board, meals, and books to try out and walk on at UTC. The lack of guarantee was very difficult for my parents, and anybody really, to understand, but I knew in my heart I was doing the right thing.

When I told my college coach I was leaving I had to get a transfer signed. She refused to sign it without a hearing. A hearing involved me, at the age of nineteen, standing in front of the University Athletic Director, my head University softball coach, the women's coordinator, the men's coordinator, my academic advisor, and my parents to explain why I was making this transition and why it was the best decision for my future.

Come to find out, I was the only person in the room who did not doubt my dream. They collectively explained to me how I was making a huge mistake. The men's coordinator and men's head basketball coach at the time explained how being a big fish in a small pond was sometimes better than being a small fish in a big pond. It was difficult to stand in a room with several adults whom I genuinely admired and to hear they did not support my goal.

Quite honestly, I was not phased. I was not leaving that hearing without a signed transfer paper and after a lot of persuading, it happened. I had my ticket for a chance to be on the field with some of the best softball players and coaches in the nation at the time.

I can still remember my parents' car driving away from my dorm after they moved me in, dropped me off, and went back home to San Antonio. I got moved in and settled. I met the coaches at the field and got my tryout.

Afterward, we spoke. They told me I had made the team but that there was no money available; at semester, we would revisit, and they would let me know if there was a change.

I played the fall season and loved every minute of the opportunities I was given. These opportunities did not just include practicing under some of the best coaches. Our grad assistant, the college player of the year, coached me at third base. I also got to meet the greats like Dani Tyler, Dot Richardson, and Lisa Fernandez and wear their gold medals. They spoke to us and shared Olympic stories. They taught us so much. It was a dream come true. It was a season that I genuinely hold so close to my heart. I learned so much, was given an opportunity, and worked very hard to ensure a spot on the field.

I cannot tell you the number of hours that went into this one season. It was what seemed like a lifetime of drills, tee work, long toss, pitching, front toss, cage work, and climbing locked fences of fields with bases left on them, just to run sixty feet over and over and over again perfecting my slide. My moment had come, and all the discouragement from the people telling me I could not do it gave me an inexplicable feeling. It was overwhelming to have accomplished a goal: one I believed in, created, and made happen myself with the help of my family.

After my time in Tennessee, I was given the opportunity to try out for the professional league, something I never imagined would happen to me. And there I went alone, driving to Palm Springs, California after work one day to take down this big dream knocking at my door.

I was still the same five-foot-two, one hundred pound kid from San Antonio who believed she could accomplish her dreams if she was just given a chance. So, I did. I believed in myself, put myself out there, and was not afraid of the challenge. I wasn't scared of the big world in front of me or even the long drive. There was nothing that could have stopped me from finding out what the softball world had in store for me.

I came up short and did not fulfill this dream. However, the experience and the opportunity shaped who I became in life from this point. Because of this experience, I became a person who was able to look fear, stress, and big situations in the face and take them head-on. I became a person who heard the word "no" and took it as a challenge, not an obstacle. I became a person who believed that I was in control of my future.

My paths were not chosen for me any longer. If I wanted something, I was going to give it my best. I would not fail because of a lack of effort. When failure did come my way, it would be to push me in the right direction on my life journey.

See, I was always a winner, no matter the adversity. I had parents who loved me, believed in me, and gave me power. They supported my strengths, acknowledged my weaknesses, and maneuvered me down a path to ensure my success. Even though I had this external support, a dream—true empowerment, the drive to accomplish what can look and feel like the impossible—lies within us. The ability to make your dreams a reality cannot be taught; it cannot be given to you by anyone. The strength that each person has to pull out of themselves is something that resides in us to our core.

No matter how many times my dad yelled at me, I was not alone on the mound. It was nine against one with my team. The power to win the at-bat, the inning, the season—it lay within me. No one else could get up there and do it for me. That strength that we need to accomplish our goals is within each of us.

You are the key to your success. You are the hero of your story. No matter how many times the world tells you no, no matter how many times you strike out, it is the getting back up, the training, the preparation, and the confidence inside of you that will allow you to accomplish your dream.

All of these moments led me to the place where I am now sharing my story and teaching others how to follow their heart, find their strength, discover their voice, and develop their work ethic. People do not always know how to stand up for themselves with grace and kindness. Still, it's important to work hard and do what is right, to love and lead with positivity.

It must be taught that positivity, kindness, and love are not signs of weakness. What do you do when coaching is not just coaching but also counseling, parenting, organizing, lecturing, and nurturing?

I have had many kids who have been through such adultlike experiences and have had to guide and assist each of them. I cannot just take care of the situation for them. It is our responsibility to teach them how to handle these situations and to provide them with strategies and plans to handle anything that comes their way.

Some experiences can be tragic. In these moments, we as leaders are never prepared, but we are grateful to be there. I once had a player whose mom died. Two days after she passed, the girl came back. When I saw her, I knelt next to her, and she could barely speak. I hugged this girl, and she could barely stand. It must've been so painful to lose the single most valuable human she knows and would ever know, her mom, just two days ago—forty-eight hours, 2,880 minutes. She could barely stand or raise her head.

Her pain weighed her down like nothing I have ever felt. I wanted to crawl into her body and be her backbone to hold her up high, but I could not do that; I could hug her and let her cry, and I could tell her to find her feet and put one foot in front of the other. I could tell her to not think and to play a game she has played her whole life, to play a game she fell in love with. If she did that, her breath would come back and her stomach would not hurt and her body would do what it has done for her the last fifteen years when she had a twelve-inch yellow ball in her hand.

And, suddenly, she did that; she walked; she threw; she hit; she dove; she played softball that day. Amid tragedy she found herself, and she thrived. For one small time in her day, she was not a victim of circumstance; she was not a girl who lost her mom. She was a player, an athlete, a third baseman, a hitter, and a teammate. Her bat and the glove that she has put on so many times gave her the strength to run.

She ran off the field three hours later sweaty, dirty, and proud, with her head high and her resilience shining through.

THIS, this moment, this is why I coach. This is why I lead. Because she showed up.

This is where she wanted and needed to be, and we needed to hold her, love her, and guide her.

These encounters, experiences, and opportunities help us to learn, get better, and to live. I am a leader, but I am led every day by people who show me what true strength and passion look like. These people remind me of why it is important to influence and inspire others. Sports are games, but athletics teaches us how to persevere, how to get through the hardest of times, and how to never give up.

Coaching reminds me those teaching athletes about the lessons of the games—are teaching the most important lessons of life. Knowing how to overcome adversity and stress gives players skills in managing difficult situations and hardships. They learn how to be bold, strong, and confident and how to achieve their best selves every chance they get. At any moment everything can be taken away and things can be different and times can be hard. It is important to be ready, to fight for what you want, and to always be your best self.

ABOUT THE AUTHOR:

Social Media:
Email welhammaggi@gmail.com

Maggi Welham is a mother to son Evan and daughter Kyle. Being a mother is her favorite leadership role in all of her career of influence. She has been in education and coaching for almost twenty years. She is a devoted daughter, sister, aunt, coach, colleague, and friend. She spends her time with her family, entertaining, reading, golfing, shopping at the Market Square or Pearl, and playing cards at home with her kids. Maggi shared her story to inspire everyone to live life honestly and without fear.

FULL CIRCLE
Manny Trujillo

There are five things that I love being called: Son, Bro, Babe, Dad, and Coach.

The Original

I can recall patiently waiting outside in the backyard for Dad to get home from work. The majority of the time, we had a game going on with cousins and neighborhood friends for whatever sport was in the season. My first love was baseball, and I enjoyed working at it. My dad would be everything that I needed in a first coach because he was a good athlete in his own right, excelling in track, baseball, and football. He was my fungo hitter, my bullpen catcher, and my batting practice thrower, and he did all of it with a smile on his face.

He never made me feel bad about myself. When coaching, he always boosted my confidence and showed me various ways to work on anything I was struggling with within the game. At the time, I took for granted how hard my dad worked throughout the day just to come home and play with me, my two older brothers, and my cousins as well. When I became a dad, I can recall coming home from work and practice being worn out, knowing that my oldest son Kade would be ready at the door with whatever ball was in season to go outside and play. I would give my wife, Kandice, a quick hug and kiss, and ask her about her day, while Kade waited patiently, just like I did as a boy. These moments had come full circle, and I became the fungo hitter, the BP thrower, the quarterback, and the soccer goalie, and I loved every minute of it, just like I realized my dad had loved being my first coach many years before.

The Impressionist

A volunteer coach is a special person because they dedicate their time to the betterment of other people's children. Plenty of the time volunteer coaches are the mom or dad of one of the players, but that is not always the case.

I was lucky enough to be coached by my uncle, Johnny Trujillo. By the time I started playing little league, he had been coaching for over ten years, and his teams had won many little league titles throughout that decade. Here is the amazing thing: even though he had three children of his own, who were involved in athletics and other school events, he was there with us. Through coaching, Uncle Johnny not only taught me about baseball, but he also taught me invaluable life lessons that have left an indelible impression on me.

I remember a time when I didn't have a very good outing on the mound, so I got pulled and moved to shortstop. I was there crying inside of my glove when I heard Uncle Johnny say, "If you don't stop crying, I'm going to sit you on the bench." I was upset because I wanted to please him, but he had to show me some tough love. As I ran toward the dugout after the inning, Uncle Johnny pulled me to the side, put his hands on my shoulders, and told me, "You can't get too high when you're up to or too low when you're down. Just stay consistent."

I can honestly say that this advice has stayed with me for thirty-eight years, and I have shared this wisdom with numerous players and students. Thank you, Tío! In addition to my Uncle Johnny, I would also like to recognize Emmett Aguirre, Fidel Serna, and Rudy

Castilleja for being such great role models for us. All of my little league coaches left a huge impression on me.

The Ceramist

A ceramist is someone who works with clay; they mold and leave their impression. I was blessed to be one of the last Trujillos in my generation to come through Hearne High School. The other blessing was that the same coaching staff had stayed there for many years. The tough part about this was there were big shoes to fill, both in the classroom and on the field/court, but I did all I could to rise to the challenge.

In high school, you begin to think about your future and what you may want to become one day. Many people struggle with this decision, but for me, I knew exactly what I wanted to do. I wanted to become a teacher/coach, and a lot of this decision was shaped by my high school coaches who meant so much to me. They pushed me to be better. Many of them graduated from Hearne High School and I could see how they went out and achieved great things. They were exceptional role models. Two coaches that really had a huge impact on me were Brian Mullinnix and Tommy Dotson.

Coach Mullinnix was a Hearne High graduate who was known to strike a lick on the football field and could do it all on the baseball diamond. He later went on to Mary Hardin Baylor to continue his athletic career in baseball. We were very lucky to have Coach Mullinnix come into the baseball program when I was a freshman. He was my freshman football and head baseball coach for four years.

We had fun, but when it was time to work, we went to work. I learned and watched him, coach, taking many tips and pointers from him, which I applied as a coach myself years later. In a full-circle moment, my oldest son Kade would later be in Coach Mullinnix's sons' class in high school.

In addition, to Coach Mullinnix's influence, Coach Tommy Dotson impacted me in countless ways. He was very soft-spoken, a true gentleman, and loved by everyone. I was blessed to be around Coach Dotson for all four years of high school. First, as a freshman in his health and driver's education class.

This man taught me how to drive, and I can still recall my first time behind the wheel. We were in the neighborhood by the local pool, and it was my turn. I set the seat, checked my mirrors, put my foot on the brake, and put the car in drive. I didn't have my foot on the accelerator and the coach said, "Give it some gas." I did as told; he said, "Take a right up here", and boy, did I. I took a sharp right turn that quickly put Coach Dotson in my lap. He kind of chuckles and says, "Dang, Manny, you have to slow down before you turn!"

Coach just had to tell me one time, and I would adjust. I was lucky enough to be coached by him on both sides of the ball in football. During the season, we spent the next three years together, and it was an awesome experience for me. The thing I loved about Coach Dotson was that he never spoke of himself as a player. He was an amazing athlete at Hearne High in football and baseball. He even went on to play baseball at Sam Houston State, where they won a national championship. Even with the accolades, Coach Dotson didn't make it about himself. It was always about his players.

Years later, I had the opportunity to have dinner with Coach Dotson and his daughter, Tara. We caught up and shared stories. I picked his brain on some coaching strategies, and we talked about the future of his grandkids and my children. I cherish this dinner because I got the opportunity to let him know just how influential he was to me. I felt comfortable in my pursuit of coaching because I had been led by him and so many other great coaches. We lost Coach Dotson a few years back, but his legacy will live on through his children, grandchildren, and all those he taught and coached.

I would also like to recognize Robert Earl Davis, Billy Ray Davis, Jimmy Reeder, and Bobby Carson as coaches who I looked up to as role models.

The Lifers

I have been blessed to work on some phenomenal coaching staffs, filled with men and women who led by example, were always prepared, and held high regard for the school, sport, and student-athletes. I know that one of the smartest things I ever did early in my coaching career was to become a sponge. By this, I mean that I would listen, take notes, ask questions, watch the extra film, come in early, and stay late.

I wanted to pick the brains of the men and women who had coached so well for all of those years. I watched how they handled players in different situations, without giving anyone special treatment. I also observed how they managed games and personnel, how they handled the officials, and how they interacted and showed respect to the other teams' coaches, players, and supporters. There is much more than the X's and O's of a sport; so much goes into getting prepared for a home or away game, and unless you have done it, it would be really hard to explain, no matter the sport.

I had the pleasure of watching and learning from some greats. There are really too many to mention by name, and I don't want to leave anyone out. Just know that if I had the pleasure of coaching with you, I learned something from you.

I have had the opportunity of coaching many great young men who went on to become exceptional husbands and fathers. I love the opportunity of catching up with a former player or seeing them succeed in life. This has been the greatest gift from coaching: the relationships.

I know that it is cliche to say, but if I positively affected at least one of my athlete's life, then I feel that all of the hard work, extra hours, and time away from family has been well worth it. I was able to take all that I learned from my dad, my uncle, my high school coaches, and my colleagues to become the best version of myself.

Special recognition goes out to all coaches' spouses, significant others, and their children.

I put my coaching whistle down ten years ago. While in many ways it was the toughest decision of my life, it was also the easiest decision that I ever made. I dearly miss the camaraderie of the coaching staff and the player interactions, but my decision was made so that I could spend more time with my family, especially my own children. I have gotten to be more present for my own kids' milestones and just become Dad.

I hope this chapter finds you well; best wishes to you and yours. It is an honor to be part of this book with so many great people.

ABOUT THE AUTHOR:

Social Media:
IG @manlawtru
FB @MannyTrujillo
Email mankantrujillo@att.net

Manny Trujillo is a second-generation teacher/coach who just completed his twenty-third year in education. He was born and raised in Hearne, Texas, where he graduated from Hearne High School. He later received his bachelor's degree in kinesiology and education from Sam Houston State University. His wife, Kandice, is also an educator with twenty-six years of teaching experience. His oldest son, Kade, is a junior, majoring in industrial distribution at Texas A&M University. His youngest son, Karson, is a sophomore at Klein Collins High School, and his only daughter, Mia, is a freshman at Klein Collins High School.

LESSONS I LEARNED FROM A WILDCAT
Royce Slechta

"You are only one decision away from a totally different life."
Mark Batterson

Driving up the gravel road leading to Wildcat Field at Lake Highlands High School was a rather surreal experience this past February. It is a drive I have made on numerous occasions and one that hasn't changed much. The most noticeable change to this baseball field that houses so many memories for me is that it is now called "Higgins Field". It is named after Jay Higgins, the baseball coaching legend of the Lake Highlands Wildcats who served as the head coach of this program for forty-three years, from 1968 until 2011.

The reason for my trip to this venue was to participate in the annual alumni baseball game. At fifty-five, while I don't run quite as well as I used to, I consider myself to be in decent shape. Serving as the offensive coordinator and quarterbacks coach at Dallas Jesuit, I would frequently jump in a drill with the guys, especially if we were shorthanded. That being said, my wife was very specific with me that morning as I got dressed about not getting hurt. It is typical for one or two older guys to get hurt while playing in a contest like this one.

At the Lake Highlands Alumni Classic, teams are divided by age, with the older guys taking on the younger ones. This event had a unique dynamic for me because I spent a few summers coaching the summer league baseball team at Lake Highlands. As a result, I found myself catching up with former teammates and players most of the day. As the game entered the last inning with the older guys leading, Coach Higgins said to me, "Hey, you haven't played today, have you?" I told him it was not that big of a deal, and he said to grab a ball and get loose and that he would bring me in to pitch in the last inning.

Fortunately for me, the mound at Higgins Field is familiar territory, having pitched there during my junior and senior years. However, since 1985, most of my experiences were with an "L" screen at the front of the mound. If you are not a baseball person it is hard to appreciate the difference between fifty-two feet, and sixty feet, six inches. It is an equally big difference as when you are wearing tennis shoes and not baseball cleats.

Not wanting to disappoint my former coach, I was up to the challenge. While I wish they could have played "Enter Sandman" for me. I made my way into the game when Coach Higgins made a rare trip to the mound and signaled for me. As he handed me the ball, he imparted forty-three years of wisdom and uttered, "Throw strikes!"

Standing on the mound as I took a few warmup pitches brought back a wave of memories, and, after a few pitches, I wasn't sure if I would be able to throw one strike! It was at that moment one of my former players from the opposing dugout shouted, "Hey, old man, why don't you take off the warmup jacket?"

That was all the "encouragement" I needed, and about fifteen pitches later, the older alumni Wildcats had a victory.

Over the next few pages, I will share with you the impact Jay Higgins has had on me as a player, coach, and more importantly, a man. Just as he handed me the ball last February along with some encouraging words, he handed me a ball with much more than that early on in my life.

"Believe you can and you are halfway there."
Theodore Roosevelt

My first encounter with Jay Higgins was at his summer baseball camp at a local city-owned field. I was one of about one hundred or so campers in attendance for this week-long event. At age eleven, this was my first instructional camp attended, and most of my baseball knowledge came from my dad, who played some semi-professional ball out of high school.

As I reflect on this camp from a coaching perspective, it was full of quality instruction, praise, competition, and even a little baseball trivia. Little did I know at the time, I would not only work at this camp as a student instructor, but I would help manage other student instructors during my last few years of working at the camp. It was during the years helping Coach Higgins run this camp that I first started to consider what it would be like to coach for a living.

For an eleven-year-old kid at his first baseball camp, I knew one thing. I wanted to play baseball for this man who seemed to know everything imaginable about the game. Little did I know, he was interested in teaching me more than just baseball, and I would learn about some of these things firsthand, in my second year of attending the camp.

"People don't care how much you know until they know how much you care."
John Maxwell

During the late seventies, I grew up in the Dallas suburb of Lake Highlands on what is affectionately known as the "L streets". If you are from Lake Highlands, then you know. While the families in this part of the neighborhood weren't exactly in the poor house, it was a neighborhood full of blue-collar folks.

Coach Higgins lived just a couple of blocks away from my house, and because my family only had one vehicle at the time, he was happy to provide a ride for me too and from the camp. As I rode for the first time in that two-door, standard Nissan truck, which also doubled as a gator to drag the baseball field, I had some of my first conversations with this baseball coaching legend. Most of the conversations we had centered around the subject of the radio message from Paul Harvey on WBAP 820, who Coach Higgins loved to listen to.

What made some of these early trips even more special is that I had a father who was gone on several sea duty trips with the U.S. Navy, and Coach Higgins would fill that void of growing up without a father figure in my life. As I have worked in the coaching profession for the last twenty-six years, I have come to appreciate the importance of coaches filling this void for many of their players.

As we traveled to the camp each morning, we would go by the high school to fill coolers with ice and Gatorade and pick up baseballs, bats, and other equipment. Sometimes we would pick up other kids on the way, and I was always glad I lived so close to Coach Higgins because the other guys had to ride in the back of the truck. On the way home from camp in the summer Texas heat, he would always stop off at the local 7/11 and buy a Slurpee or Big Gulp for everyone he was driving.

I am reminded of those stops at the convenience store to this day each time I stop at one with my family. The importance of taking care of the people closest to you is one of the firsthand lessons I learned from him.

"You can't be a great leader if all you are serving is yourself."
Jon Gordon

When I was a sophomore, and finally got to Lake Highlands High School, I had become a seasoned veteran of the Baseball Skills and Drills Camp. I felt very confident in my chances of making the team. I spent most of my early years as a catcher, and when I got to the varsity team we already had two older catchers on the team.

During my sophomore season I was somewhat of a utility player; catching, playing outfield, designated hitter, etc. That season I learned the importance of players to know their role on the team and to do their best when called upon to play. Our team made it to the regional finals that year, and we would return to the same level again during my junior year.

One of the biggest physical attributes I was blessed with was arm strength, and Coach Higgins asked me to do some pitching my junior year. As a pitcher, I started to understand more about the game from calling pitches to the importance of ball location and how to take advantage of opposing hitters. During this season, with the help of some pretty talented players, I was able to earn all-district honors as a pitcher. I pitched in some playoff games as well.

When you play as far into the post-season as we played those two years, you spend some time traveling on road trips. Many times on these road trips, Coach Higgins would bring his daughters Jaime and Joy to travel with us. I'm not sure what prompted me initially, other than coming from a caring home, but I felt the need to make these road trips for the girls more tolerable, so I started reading to them. Looking back on the experience, it stands to reason I would soon spend my professional career as an educator. I think Coach Higgins was thankful to have someone spend time with his daughters, but I also think it was a time when he realized I was someone he could trust.

Joy and Jayme Higgins – 1984

I think I was the natural choice out of all the other guys on the team because of the previous relationship I had with Coach Higgins. A few years later that I would even house sit for him when his family went on vacation, and even though I followed specific instructions, I managed to always turn their pool green! After high school, my relationship with my coach would grow even more, and I would find myself making a decision that would change the course of my life.

"Everyone wants to be great, until it's time to do what greatness requires."
Joshua Medcalf

Along with playing baseball in high school, I was fortunate enough to play football at East Texas State University and West Texas State University. During the summer before transferring to West Texas State, Coach Higgins asked me if I would be interested in coaching his summer baseball team. I gladly accepted, and whether it was the success we had that summer, or simply because he believed in me, I felt this was without question what I wanted to do for the rest of my life.

"If you want God to do the super, you've got to do the natural."
Mark Batterson

I finished my playing career in the fall of 1990 and was on track to serve as a student assistant with the football program at West Texas State, but, due to some internal issues, the football program was dropped for the 1991 season. That same year, I was approached by the dean of students about starting a baseball club program. She noticed a baseball camp T-shirt I was wearing that day and that is what prompted her.

Although my career has had more defining moments, this is one I reflect on with the biggest sense of pride and accomplishment. Starting a baseball program from scratch involves a ton of work, but I felt confident in my ability because of the knowledge Coach

Higgins had imparted to me. The baseball program at West Texas A&M University is now part of the athletic program, and I feel as though I played an integral role in the process.

During the spring of 1992, along with changing the school name to West Texas A&M University, the school administration decided to bring back the football program, and I was hired as a graduate assistant. It was during this first year I actually coached a very young Chip Baker, that's right, the same Chip Baker who is the author of this great series of books, *The Impact of Influence.*

I went on to become a full-time assistant at West Texas A&M after that season, and officially launched my career as a coach. Although my career has been centered on football, it is the lessons I learned from Coach Higgins that helped to develop me into the coach I am today. For the last thirty-seven years, I have either had a phone conversation or an in-person visit with Coach Higgins each of those years.

Jay Higgins was inducted into the THSCA Hall of Fame in 2010, retired from coaching in 2011, and to this day drives a bus for athletic programs at Lake Highlands when they travel for games. I am sure some young student-athletes riding in the bus he drives have no idea of all of his accomplishments.

If I learned anything from Coach Higgins over the years it is the importance of being a servant leader. As I enter the last few years of my coaching career, it is what I have tried to impart to the players I have coached. Coach Higgins taught with values of loyalty, integrity, accountability, perseverance, trust, and respect, and he impressed on me the importance of relationships.

Tony Dungy, in his book, *Mentor Leader* (Tyndale House Publishers. Carol Stream, Illinois. August 2010), talks about the 7 E's of enhancing potential when it comes to leadership and mentoring, and Coach Higgins was certainly my biggest mentor.

These steps for enhancing potential from Coach Dungy are listed below:

- **Engage** – It is critical for coaches to engage with players. Without it, you cannot lead effectively.
- **Educate** – The first step in creating leaders, after engaging with those you lead, is to educate.
- **Equip** – Equipping is providing to proper resources and tools – physical, mental, spiritual, and emotional – for the team to be successful.
- **Encourage** – Nothing does more to lubricate the rough spots than encouragement.
- **Empower** – Preparation followed by appropriate freedom.
- **Energize** – Great coaches energize and inspire the players they coach.
- **Elevate** – Build leaders who will lead elsewhere. Especially multi-sport athletes.

Today, we live in a very technological world, especially after a pandemic stripped us of opportunities to spend with each other face to face. I have tried to embrace this unique situation as a coach and meet players where they live and on their devices.

Over recent years I have started working on broadening my knowledge base, and have become much more of a reader than ever before. As I grow spiritually and professionally, I share many of the things I come across with players I coach, co-workers, and friends I have developed throughout my life. This new journey has become what some might call an obsession with my reading between thirty or forty books in the last year alone.

I have seen quite a few things over the last twenty-five-plus years of my coaching career, and I feel it important to continue to develop as a leader and a child of God.

In closing, there is a recent quote I would like to share with you from Mark Batterson's book, *Soul Print:* "Sometimes the blessings we enjoy are not the by-product of anything we have done. Sometimes they are the by-product of someone's faithfulness generations ago, and that person's faithfulness nets blessings decades after he or she has died."

Below is a list of several things I've read over the last few years that have become a big part of who I am now. It is my prayer you will find some of these to be a blessing for you as well.

"You are never too old to set another goal, or to dream a new dream."
C.S. Lewis

Blessings,
Royce Slechta
Romans 8:28

Spiritual Books/Author
Crazy Love/ Francis Chan, *Play the Man*/Mark Batterson, *Intentional Living*/John Maxwell, *Chase the Lion*/Mark Batterson, *Forgotten God*/Francis Chan, *Win the Day*/Mark Batterson, *Uncommon*/Tony Dungy, *Do It For a Day*/ Mark Batterson, *Lead For God's Sake*/Todd Gongwer, *Double Blessing*/Mark Batterson, *Goliath Must Fall*/ Louis Giglio, *All In*/Mark Batterson, *If*/ Mark Batterson, *Never Too Far*/Louis Giglio, *Whisper*/Mark Batterson, *The Circle Maker*/Mark Batterson, *You and Me Forever*/Francis Chan

Leadership Books/Author
Burn Your Goals/Joshua Medcalf, *Mindset*/Carol Dweck, *A Leader's Heart*/John Maxwell, *Take the Stairs*/Rory Vaden, *Failing Forward*/John Maxwell, T*ransformational Leadership*/Joshua Medcalf, *The 17 Indisputable Laws of Teamwork*/John Maxwell, *The Power of Positive Leadership*/Jon Gordon, *Grit*/ Angela Duckworth, *Pound the Stone*/Joshua

Medcalf, *Drive*/Daniel Pink, *The Power of a Positive Team*/ Jon Gordon, *The Twin Thieves*/Lucas Jadin, *Fortitude*/Dan Crenshaw, *Win In The Dark*/Joshua Medcalf, *The Leadership Handbook*/John Maxwell, *The Energy Bus*/ Jon Gordon, *Smarter Faster Better*/Charles Duhigg, *Developing the Leader Within You*/John Maxwell, *Mentor Leader*/ Tony Dungy, *360 Degree Leader*/John Maxwell, *Chop Wood Carry Water*/Joshua Medcalf, *The Power of Full Engagement*/Jim Loehr, *The 21 Irrefutable Laws of Leadership*/John Maxwell, *Inside Out Coaching*/ Joe Ehrmann, *The Only Way to Win*/Jim Loehr, *Change Your World*/John Maxwell, *What Drives Winning*/Brett Ledbetter

ABOUT THE AUTHOR:

Social Media:
IG @RoyceSlechta
FB @RoyceSlechta
Email rslechta@jesuitcp.org

This past season in 2021, Coach Slechta coordinated an offense that finished in the top ten in the DFW metroplex (435 ypg, 40 ppg) while the Rangers finished as 7-6A District Champions with a 10-2 record.

In 2019, Slechta helped power the Rangers to the state quarterfinal for the first time in program history, behind an offense that averaged 33 points per game while closing the year with over 5,200 yards of total offense. As quarterbacks' coach, Slechta coached quarterback Rance Holman '20 to a 2,385-yard season, which included 21 passing touchdowns over 14 games. The Jesuit offense paved the way for the running back tandem of E.J. Smith '20, and rising senior Jake Taylor to combine for 2,025 yards and 30 touchdowns.

In 2018, Wylie captured a bi-district championship, the first since the Pirates entered Class 6A in 2016. The Pirates averaged 360 yards per game, anchored by quarterback Rashad Dixon, who was named the District 10-6A Most Valuable Player after finishing the season with 3,030 yards and 36 touchdowns. Wylie's offense was consistently ranked as one of the best in the area by the Dallas Morning News, and Slechta was a part of Wylie's state semifinalist team in 2010, state quarterfinalist in 2013, a regional semi-finalist in 2015, as well as bi-district champions in 2012 and 2014.

Throughout his 25-year career in athletics, Slechta has coached student-athletes throughout Texas at the high school and collegiate levels. He held his first position at West Texas A&M University as the quarterbacks and receivers coach from 1992-to 97. During the 1994 season, the Buffalos led the nation in total offense (571 ypg), passing (455 ypg), and scoring (46 ppg). Slechta also worked at

Dalhart, Gainesville, Tascosa, Newman Smith, and Sherman before arriving in Wylie for the 2010 season. Slechta has enjoyed success at each of his stops, including a district championship with Gainesville in 2000, a district-leading offense with Newman Smith in 2005, and one of the area's best offenses in Class 4A during his four-year tenure in Sherman.

Slechta graduated from West Texas A&M in 1993 with a bachelor's degree in education with certifications in kinesiology, history, and health. He added a master's degree in health and physical education in 1994 before beginning his professional career. An alumnus of Lake Highlands High School, Coach Slechta lives in the DFW Metroplex with his wife Carrie and daughter Sybil.

A RAM IN THE BUSH
Tamika Newman

When I reflect back on my childhood, I think of growing up in a big family and all the good and bad that come with that. However, I can't help but think about how much time we spent together at church. Being raised by Christian grandparents in the southern part of the country attending church services was a non-negotiable, one that I didn't particularly rebel against. I accepted Christ at eight-years-old.

As a Sunday school student, I'm familiar with most of The Bible stories and parables. There's one story that I love. It's the story of the ram in the bush from Genesis 22.

God commanded Abraham to sacrifice his son and, just as he was about to obey God and kill his son, he heard a ram rustling in the bushes. He then used the ram as a sacrifice instead of his son. There are tons of takeaways, but I've always gleaned this: if we do our part as God commands us to do, He will always provide.

I believed this scripture with my whole heart even as a kid. Despite what I could see in my environment, I trusted that the Lord would provide a way for me to accomplish my dreams.

When I was about twelve years old, I decided that I was going to be an elite athlete like the WNBA players who I saw running up and down the court in the inaugural season of the league or like the long athletic women who played for the US National Volleyball Team. I had no idea how I was going to achieve this, so I set out on the path toward these goals, creating my own blueprint on the way.

Middle-school sports came, and I worked hard but didn't show very much promise initially. By the end of the eighth grade, I was five-foot-eight had played volleyball, basketball, and track both seasons, and I wasn't half bad. I spent the entire summer on my neighborhood blacktop court playing basketball against the guys; girls very rarely showed up to play. My basketball skills grew exponentially.

As a high school freshman, I was on the freshman volleyball, varsity basketball, and junior varsity track teams. I was locked in on my goal of being an elite athlete. At this time, I was starting to realize that I needed to earn an athletic scholarship. I started paying attention to college basketball games and fell in love with the University of Texas Longhorns.

Starting the summer after ninth grade, I rose bright and early every morning to make the mile-long trek to my high school to participate in the strength and conditioning program. I was the only female athlete to do so. I figured, that if I couldn't afford to play on the travel volleyball or basketball teams, then I could at least train for free at the school to be faster and stronger than my opponents. The unwanted attention from the guys was uncomfortable, but it was a price I had to pay.

A player transferred in my sophomore year who had an involved dad. They started a small travel basketball team with some of the girls from the school team. We were so grateful for the opportunity to play, and it didn't cost our parents much money.

In the next few years, I believe God sent several people on my path that helped me to get closer to my goal of earning an athletic scholarship to college. I even got to play on a real AAU travel basketball team that was sponsored by someone from NASA.

Senior year rolled around, and no college coaches were showing any interest in me. I grew concerned but continued working hard in practice, in the weight room, and on the court.

The volleyball program broke a thirteen-year streak of not making the state playoffs that fall. The basketball team that hadn't made it in twenty years was on the verge of doing the same.

One winter afternoon, I came home to find I had a message from the basketball coach at Prairie View A&M University. PVAMU is a small public agriculture university fifty miles northwest of Houston. I had heard of it briefly but didn't know much. I called back Coach Jerald Moore, who had gotten a hold of some film of me playing basketball and thought I would be a great fit for the program.

The only thing was I had set an audacious goal of playing both basketball and volleyball in college. I asked him if they had any two-sport athletes at the university. He responded by telling me in previous years there had been and that he would follow up with the volleyball coach to see if she would allow it.

Within a few days, I received a call from Alicia Pete, head volleyball coach at PVAMU. She began the conversation by telling me that she had received a call from someone telling her about my play. I don't remember much of the conversation after that except she was very open to me playing both sports and invited me down for an official visit to tour the campus.

In the late spring of 2004, I signed a National Letter of Intent to play basketball and volleyball at Prairie View A&M University. My family was elated, and I couldn't believe it. I was the first person in my family to receive any kind of scholarship to college and the first multi-sport college athlete at my high school.

My excitement would be short-lived because volleyball training camp the following August would prove to be very difficult. The adjustment to living alone, my teammates, coaches, and the academic workload was overwhelming. Basketball season was much of the same. My sophomore year rolled around, and I didn't make any noise in any sport; in fact, I decided to quit basketball and just pursue volleyball for the remainder of my time on campus.

During junior year, I showed up with a renewed sense of purpose ready to give all of my effort to volleyball and academics. This recommitment paid off as we won the Southwestern Athletic

Conference that season, automatically granting us admittance into the NCAA Volleyball Tournament. As we waited to see who we would play with, Coach Alicia Pete informed us the program had only won the SWAC two times, once in 1991, coached by Jocelyn Adams, and once in 1999, coached by Pete herself.

Coach Pete casually said that Jocelyn Adams was the person who told her about me. Wow, I finally knew who that "somebody" was. She had been my "ram in the bush". I'm ashamed to admit that I didn't investigate to learn more about her at the time.

I wouldn't call her a psychic, but Coach Adams's prediction that I could play college volleyball was right. She saw something in me that I didn't see in myself because, after that freshman year volleyball season, I was ready to transfer. Thank God I didn't because I finished my career as a Southwestern Athletic Conference Team Champion my junior year and SWAC player of the year my senior year. Eventually, my team would be inducted into the Prairie View Hall of Fame.

Several years later, Coach Adams was named the new head volleyball coach at Texas Southern University in Houston. I read the news release announcing the hire and read all the things she accomplished as a student-athlete and a coach; she was a part of the Historical Track Program at PVAMU, which received national attention, and then eventually became a volleyball coach where she was successful as well.

After finally meeting in person, she explained to me that she was a middle school coach my senior year of high school and just so happened to be watching a game that I was playing in and made the call to Alicia Pete to suggest that she look into getting me on the team. She appeared right before I thought my dream might not be realized despite my praying fervently to God every day and doing my part by working hard.

Coach Adam's phone call had changed my entire life, and I could only think of one way to repay her. When I decided to be a teacher and a coach, I prided myself in finding hidden treasures in athletes. When other teachers and coaches thought certain kids were a lost cause or weren't that talented, I saw something in them and did everything in my power to pour into them and connect them to others who could as well.

As a high school coach, I made calls to college coaches for players on my team and other teams. I encouraged discouraged players and parents who didn't think college was in their future. I have a special affinity for helping kids from low resources like myself who I know just need a chance to prove themselves.

My purpose in life is to be a "ram in the bush" for as many young people as I can.

I Can.

I Will.

Watch Me.

ABOUT THE AUTHOR:

Social Media:
IG @gga_2019
FB @tamika.newman.7
Email newmantamika38@gmail.com

Shattering the glass ceiling, setting a new standard, leading the way, and winning best describe Tamika R. Newman's journey. She is a native Houstonian and one of five siblings born to her mother. Tamika's passion for sports and desire to help students in underserved communities has kept her in education for over a decade.

Tamika is the owner of Grit and Grind Athletics LLC, an athletic service provider. As a consultant, she helps sports organizations and athletic departments make sure their coaches and support staff are delivering service that aligns with their vision and promise. On the coaching side, she gives female minority coaches the tools and strategies to redefine their careers so they win at work and home through her online group coaching program, "A Coach Redefined" She also enjoys speaking to sports teams and organizations about personal development.

Tamika holds a Bachelor of Communications and a Master's in Business Administration. She is a former multi-sport athlete and graduate of Prairie View A&M University where she's in the athletics Hall of Fame and Texas Southern University. Tamika is the author of *Grateful & Greedy: Challenging and Redefining what it means to win in Life,* co-author of *Athlete to Entrepreneur and A "Champion" Redefined.*

LESSONS LEARNED THROUGH SPORTS
Taylor Cobb

When Chip first asked if I would like to contribute to his next book involving coaches, I jumped at the opportunity. It wasn't until he sent the writing prompt that I realized how difficult this was going to be. The prompt was straightforward, write about how someone or something impacted you in your life in sports/coaching, the lessons you learned from it, and how you are using it to make a positive difference in the world. It wasn't that the prompt was confusing or unclear. It was crystal clear. My difficulty was in picking one someone or something that impacted me.

There are so many impactful people and events that shaped me into the person I am today. So rather than share one person or event, I am going to do my best to share the many people and experiences that made me into the coach and person I am today.

I grew up playing little league baseball and football. I had many coaches that helped me develop athletically and personally, but I am going to skip ahead to my experiences and coaches in high school. I grew up in the same house until I went to college, so I knew what high school I was going to attend from a very early age.

One of my neighbors was a coach at the high school, and he would take me and his sons up to the school from time to time. I was in awe of the players lifting weights or doing drills on the practice field and enjoyed getting to meet and talk to the high school coaches. It was as if I was getting to meet Coach Bear Bryant or Vince Lombardi every time I met one of the coaches. This is really what started my drive to want to become a coach.

As I got older and got into high school, there were three coaches that I looked up to who helped shape me not only as a player but as a coach today. The first person was my offensive line coach, Chris Camerino. He was the type of coach that was easy to like but hard to please. He had high expectations for his players but he also made you want to reach those expectations. I remind myself constantly of this lesson: a player will only let you push them as far as the level of trust you have built with them. We always joked in the locker room that it was right of passage to get ripped or yelled at in front of the team in practice by Coach Camerino.

I remember the day, not particularly what I did wrong but that didn't matter at the time. I said, "Yes sir", and got back in the huddle. I didn't give an excuse or try to justify that what I did was right. Looking back, I believe that he was just trying to see what we would do in that situation because those that took ownership and responsibility for their actions were never publicly ripped again. I made sure to respond the same way throughout my playing career to a coach's correction.

The next coach that had an impact on me in high school was John Whitehead. He was our offensive coordinator and I also had him as my teacher in speech class. Coach Whitehead was what would be called today a "player's coach". He was a very personable coach that made sure his players understood that he not only cared for them as players but as people too. He connected to so many players from different backgrounds and was able to find common ground to build relationships.

Coach Whitehead was a big reason I decided that teaching and coaching were what I wanted to dedicate my life to. It was after school one day in the offseason that the realization hit me like a lightning bolt. A few players and I were sitting in the locker room after lifting weights and Coach Whitehead came in to see what we were doing. He came in, asked about our day, joked around with us, and then left to go to softball practice. As soon as he walked out of the door it hit me: he gets to make a living doing this, and I want to do this every day.

It wasn't just the love of playing the sport or being able to scheme up a play that could win the game that was the most appealing. It was the comradery of people coming together from different backgrounds to reach a common goal. We could put our differences aside in pursuit of something bigger than each individual and that is truly a remarkable accomplishment. That was the impact that football had on me in high school and led me down the path I am on today.

Midway through my senior season at Oak Ridge High School, we were having a great year on the football field. We were 5-0 and we started to have that feeling where we knew something special was going to happen that year. It was the very next game that I sustained a knee injury and was unsure if I was going to be able to finish the year. I still remember laying on the field and thinking to myself, "Why now? We've put so much work in. We're about to do something great."

I was really angry at myself for getting injured and not being able to be out on the field with my teammates. It was the first major injury that I had experienced so I really didn't know how to handle it. I would have most likely denied it at the time but to say I was depressed would have been an understatement. This is where the comradery of my teammates and coaches showed me the true impact that this sport can have on an individual. They were there when I needed them the most and got me to refocus on the things that I could do to help our team achieve the success that we were striving for.

Shortly thereafter, I received news that I could rehab my knee and be able to finish the season in a brace; it was some of the best news I could have received. I got to work right away in the training room and, with the help of my teammates and coaches, I was able to come back in two weeks and finish the season. That football season was the best in school history. We made the playoffs and advanced to the semifinal game.

I currently am coaching at my alma mater, Oak Ridge High School. I spent the previous ten years of my career coaching at two different high schools and was able to work with coaches that were graduates of the school. I always thought it was a really unique experience but didn't see a future where I was going to have that opportunity. But much like coaching in general, you never know what is going to happen.

I was afforded the chance to come back to Oak Ridge, and I jumped at the opportunity. I had spent the first eighteen years of my life in the Oak Ridge area, and as it ended up, spent the next eighteen years in other places. It was a blessing to come back home and give back to a school and community that had done so much for me and my family. I get to walk the halls every day and remember the experiences that I had here—some positive, some negative, but I learned from all of them.

The next coach that had a lasting impact on me not only as a coach but as a person was Dan Eason. Coach Eason was my strength and conditioning coach at Stephen F. Austin University. After my injury in my senior season, I didn't' have many scholarship opportunities to go play at the next level so I decided to walk on. For the first two years of my college career, I played at the University of Houston. I was able to make the travel team my redshirt freshman year and was able to play in a couple of games, but it never really felt like home.

I decided to transfer and had a friend that was a student at Stephen F. Austin, so I decided to drive up to visit him and the school. I really enjoyed the campus and atmosphere, so I decided to transfer there. I reached out to the current offensive line coach about an opportunity to play. He responded that the coaching staff had just been let go so he didn't know what was going to happen. I had already enrolled in school so I just had to hope that the new coaching staff would give me an opportunity to play.

Thankfully that opportunity came, and one of the first coaches I met was Coach Eason. I could tell from our first conversation it was going to take a lot to win him over. Not all walk-on athletes have a high work ethic or skill set, so sometimes coaches don't think that they should be there. I got that feeling during our first encounter with Coach Eason, but I found out later how wrong I was.

The first couple of weeks, I kept my mouth shut and just tried to out-work the hardest worker in the room at all times. Coach Eason slowly started to see that I was going to show up every day and put in the work. I did the same thing when football season rolled around, and the football coaches took notice as well. I was awarded a full scholarship and played my final three seasons at Stephen F. Austin.

Over those three years, I realized that my first encounter with Coach Eason was pretty standard for him. It wasn't that I was a walk-on, he just wanted to see how I was going to respond. Coach Eason wasn't a football coach, but he was the best coach I ever had. He had the same qualities as Coach Camerino and Coach Whitehead. He had high expectations and he held you accountable to them. He also cared about you as a person and knew how to push you to be a better version of yourself.

When I think of what coaching is really all about, it comes down to building trust to push people beyond their current ability. I strive every day to keep that in perspective. Everyone in coaching wants the most talented players, but it doesn't always work out that way. Not everyone can be naturally gifted, but everyone can improve. A good coach can get an athlete to consistently push themselves out of their comfort zone and improve themselves. This is one of the most rewarding aspects of being a coach.

When I was finished playing football, Coach Eason offered me a position as a graduate assistant strength and conditioning coach. I jumped at the opportunity to be able to work and learn more from Coach Eason. Those were some of the most exhausting yet rewarding days early in my coaching career. I learned not only about weight lifting and running programs but also how to engage and motivate athletes. I use what I learned from Coach Eason every day.

I really appreciate Chip allowing me to contribute to this book. There were so many people and experiences in sports that shaped me into the person I am today. These were just a few that stick out, but there are many more that I could have written about.

I try to remind myself when the days seem long and I get caught up in the wins and losses of what this profession is really about: helping other people achieve their goals, even when sometimes they lose sight of them.

ABOUT THE AUTHOR:

Social Media:
Email tcobb52@gmail.com

Coach Cobb is entering his fourteenth year of coaching. He is a graduate of Oak Ridge High School where he was a team captain of the 2002 State Semi-Finalist Team. He attended Stephen F. Austin University where he was a two-time All-Conference player for the Lumberjacks. After completing his undergraduate degree, Coach Cobb was a graduate assistant working with football and strength and conditioning while earning his master's degree in education. He has also made coaching stops at San Antonio East Central and Conroe High School, where he has served as both assistant head coach and offensive coordinator. Coach Cobb will be teaching economics at Oak Ridge. He has been married to his wife, Amy, since 2018. They have a two-and-a-half-year-old son, Willam, and an eight-month-old daughter, Madison.

WINS & LESSONS: SHAMGAR'S PRINCIPLE
Tyrone Void, Jr.

Sports are a microcosm of life. Athletics play a vital role in many aspects of life in streets, neighborhoods, homes, and housing projects across the globe.

As a youngster with dreams of being a professional athlete, it was natural for me to follow the examples of those I wanted to be like. Unfortunately, I didn't have the money to buy the sneakers, and I yapped too much to chew gum and wag my tongue while playing, but I wore number twenty-three and practiced my version of gravity-defying layups enough to attempt to model my game after the greatest player of my lifetime, Michael Jordan.

As my basketball career progressed and then ended unceremoniously, I was left both figuratively and literally with a single question: WHAT NOW?

During a chance meeting at a random travel basketball game in Austin, Texas in 2006, I began training basketball athletes. I would drive an hour to South Austin from my hometown of Copperas Cove sometimes twice a week to train affluent kids in the Westlake area. I became a distant, adopted, ethnically diverse cousin to that wonderful family. Somehow, I went from just a dude that trained their son at his full court in the backyard, to a guy that ate dinner with the family.

As serendipity would have it, one of the young men had a father in the medical field that noticed me favoring my aching wrist and suggested I see a specialist. Through a litany of tests, a specialist named Dr. Stephanie Booth was able to inform me that my aches were due to rheumatoid arthritis. Keep that in mind as we continue onward.

Despite the physical struggles brought on by RA and it stripping my ability to play basketball, my budding training career added gasoline that reignited a fire that had never completely subsided. After flailing around in various jobs while continuing to train, I got into coaching at a professional level at Cinco Ranch High School in Katy, Texas. As much as I worked to emulate everything down to the mannerisms and gestures that the best the game of basketball had to offer, the most influence on my game, both on and off the court, came from tangible beings. I was more affected by the players and coaches I could see and converse with than the ones I saw on television. With that in mind, I set off into my coaching and teacher career without a clue of what I was actually doing, but with intentions to make an impact similar to what had been made on me.

I learned very quickly that the X's and O's were the smallest percentages of the job. It became almost immediately apparent that the moniker of "coach" carries a weight that the most scientific scale could not detect. There was no preparation for the stoicism needed or the distinct balance I had to find between knocking knuckleheads and maneuvering the fragility of developing teenage brains. Fortunately, those days of training spent in the backyard of a Texas Hill Country home gave me the familiarity to deal with a basketball team that had only two players that looked like me. What it didn't provide, however, were the skills necessary to keep my personal emotions intact when the outcomes didn't match the effort that I felt I was applying.

Coaching the sophomore team, which is the equivalent of an upperclassman third squad or C-team in Texas High School basketball, really tested my ability to convey my basketball knowledge. In fairness to those young men, they were asked to do things that they previously were not asked to do. At this juncture in their short basketball careers, they had fully believed in their shortcomings more than any level of ability they had. After a few months together, one thing was clear, I couldn't simply tell them what I knew and expect it to translate to them carrying out my wishes. That was the very first valuable lesson I learned about my impact as a coach and how it transfers to real life.

Expertise is useless without the ability to adjust. This means that I could have told them a million things they were doing wrong. I could have, and often did, admonish them for not being able to execute on allegedly simple tasks. I would ask them why they would do this or why they didn't do that when the answer was simple: they didn't know how to do it. Plain and simple. Deeper than that, however, no previous coach had ever taken the time to explain to them the importance of knowing how to do these things. Out of self-preservation, they leaned into what they were even minimally good at. Therefore, it didn't matter how much I yelled, screamed, or made them run lines, they couldn't do it. Whether from lack of practice or true inability, what I was asking of them was not available.

Once that realization hit, I was faced with two options: continue to push against the immovable object of a nominal skillset or employ what is known as Shamgar's Principle taught to me out of the Bible via tape recordings of the late, great Bishop Nathaniel Holcomb of Christian House of Prayer.

That principle states: start where you are, use what you have, and do what you can.

Where we were was smack dab in the middle of a season. What we had was a group who played as hard as they possibly could every chance they got. I still had to incorporate the third bullet in Shamgar's Principle: do what you can—for the remainder of the season. I began to focus on how I could build upon the strengths they had while enhancing their weaknesses as much as I could.

The answer to that question, I discovered, ended up being more of a journey than a destination. In the middle of peak frustration for me, my team was relegated to practicing in the backup dance room.

But instead of practicing, we sat in a circle at the makeshift half-court and talked.

Initially, my frustration seeped into my line of questioning. I abruptly asked, "What's the issue?" More importantly, that meeting gave me a tool I would use throughout my career, and for the rest of my life.

Reflecting back, I could tell that the feelings of embarrassment, shame, and inadequacy that they had become accustomed to had made their way into this. Frustration and fear can be combustible elixirs. Psychology tells us that both emotions have a variety of ways to manifest themselves. In this case, both emotions showed up but remained quiet. The silence seemed to have lasted an hour before I took the initiative of changing my tone and reassuring them that this meeting has no bearing on their playing time or how I feel about them.

Once that ice was broken, the boys on the team, almost unanimously, felt the burden of trying to do things right. More specifically, they felt the anxiety of trying to do things perfectly. I remember very clearly one of the players saying, "Coach, it's like you think we're messing up on purpose. I promise you, we are trying our best." I saw nods of agreement across the room. He continues, "Really Coach, we just don't want to disappoint you. We really want to make you proud. It just seems like that's impossible."

I would be lying if I said my visceral internal reaction wasn't a callous one. What did they want; all smiles and hugs? We were losing. There is no fun in that. I would be less disappointed if they did what I asked. And I'm proud of them. Why wouldn't I be? They should know that.

I was mildly offended.

All of these thoughts flooded the seven-second pause between the end of that player's bold expressions and my first words. As I opened my mouth to speak, somehow my scathing thoughts produced flowery words.

"I'm sorry."

That is all I could think to say. From there, I had to still incorporate the third bullet in Shamgar's Principle: do what you can. I made it a point to verbally reassure them that I was proud of them. I never relented my expectations. I told them I would never undermine their potential as young men by allowing them to get away with things that weren't beneficial to them. What I adjusted, though, was my delivery from player to player. I began to focus on how I could use their strengths and not harp on their weaknesses.

"Do what you can."

I became more aware of how my words and interactions affected each individual. More importantly, that meeting gave me a tool I would use throughout my career. That tool was to seek more information. As a coach, I learned to ask what they were trying to do, what they saw, and did they understand what they were supposed to do. That conversation in that dance gym set the trend of open communication that increased my information, which made me a more impactful coach and leader. Not because I could place them in more advantageous situations but because they were empowered. Their voices mattered. It was no longer Coach Void providing all the answers; it was us knowing the predetermined desired result but now understanding that our path to arriving at that point would be based on our abilities to navigate solutions as a unit.

That is not something I thought about as a player. I didn't think about it, but it existed as a norm on the teams I played on coming up. My father was my first coach. He rarely yelled, but his expectations were crazy high. My high school coach, Benny Ward, cursed me out more than anybody in my entire life up to that point and beyond. However, each man allowed me the space to have a role in the process outside of just being an "X" or "O." Unbeknownst to me, that stuck with me and molded what would be my coaching style and life approach, which became based on my idea that unwavering expectations are the foundation for consistent execution

After one year at Cinco Ranch, my career took me across the proverbial tracks to Klein Forest High School as an assistant coach. I left Klein Forest after three successful years. Following a season as the number-one team in the state for the majority of the year, and lost in the last second of the regional finals game, missing the state tourney (which I still think we would have easily won). I landed as the inaugural head basketball coach at Klein Cain High School in just my fifth year as a coach. It only took one open gym to see that I had a ton of work to do.

We played strictly Junior Varsity in our first year as a program and fared well. We won fifty percent of our games before going into our first season as a competitor in Texas high schools' top classification.

Knowing what I have shared, you would think that I simply tapped back into the Shamgar principle. I did not. I began the year intending to remain positive. I would even share with parents that there would be "no losses, just lessons." I was faced with the challenge of having to live that quote to a level I hadn't bargained for ultimately.

We won two games that year. Two. It wasn't good. I found myself wallowing in the frustration that I felt in the middle of my first year. I wasn't used to losing anymore. We had lost more games in a row than I had lost in three previous years combined. However, the scoreboard wasn't where I lost the most. I had lost my focus. I allowed my competitive fire to burn away my purpose for coaching and to understand the larger picture of the impact I was having on these young men's life experiences. I let basketball and the self-imposed pressure it provided overtake the "lessons" we were to derive from such a tough season.

After the year was over, I had time to reflect. We had our chances to win several games, but my relationship with the boys set the tone for chaos to ensue. I broke multiple clipboards and conducted myself embarrassingly to officials for all to see. Stepping back from it and ultimately going to administration, I felt empty. I knew that wasn't the best representation of who I was or wanted to be. I loved the boys, and we stuck to the code I had previously implemented of high expectations off the court. I fell short by not showing them my appreciation of their effort and, quite frankly, tolerance of my shortcomings. I also failed to course-correct using Shamgar's Principle. I became a better coach that offseason, though I wouldn't coach at that level again.

The "lesson" I ended up learning instead of teaching is one of the processes: the joy of the process. In life, there is an ultimate battle being fought. Within this larger battle, it is important to find situational victories. Coaching has taught me that having a team that trusts you enough to execute a play to perfection means more than if they make or miss the shot that derives from that play. The trust that led to that execution is the victory. The shot going in or not is a function of many things, but the unit pulling together to make that shot available is the situational victory that narrows down the work that needs to be done. Now, analogously speaking, we do not have to worry about the many moving parts that go into getting the play correct. We can focus on practicing the shot.

That's the difference. My two toughest seasons as a coach taught me the most. I had to learn that unwavering expectations are unfair unless explained, and my alleged expertise means nothing if it isn't coupled with the understanding that adjustment is necessary. Those young men that I was able to coach have impacted my life more than I could have imagined. I now lead and parent from the place of one victory at a time. It doesn't matter if it is a large win or a personal accomplishment. The wins are in the process.

Inspect with introspection FIRST!
Critique with care.
Admonish with awareness.
Employ expertise with room for expansion.

That is our job as coaches, leaders, and people. We are charged to pull the very best out of each other. Then, and only then, can we expect the same in return. It doesn't matter what we think we "should be." We can only deal with what "currently is."

Start where you are. Use what you have. Do what you can.

ABOUT THE AUTHOR:

Social Media:
IG @tjvoid
FB @childrensbooksbytyronevoid
Email tyronevoidjr@gmail.com

Tyrone Void, Jr, more widely known as TJ, is a husband and a father. He has dedicated a large portion of his life to the advancement of others. A former athlete, he initially poured himself into the sport of basketball. After college, and once basketball was over, Tyrone spent time in sales and as a staff writer for Nicekicks.com before entering his current career in education.

Tyrone began his career at Cinco Ranch High School, teaching English 1 and serving as an assistant coach in 2013. After a year, he moved on to Klein Forest High School, again teaching English 1 and serving as an assistant coach for a year before moving up to the associate position. While there, Tyrone helped lead Klein Forest's boy's basketball team to a record thirty-four game winning streak, a #1 State Ranking, and a run to the State Regional Finals.

He left Klein Forest and became the very first head boys basketball coach at Klein Cain High School. While at Cain, Tyrone won campus and district Secondary Teacher of the Year in 2019. He left the sidelines to become the assistant principal following in 2019 and now serves as the Dean of Administration at Klein Intermediate, where he recently won campus AP of the Year in 2022.

Throughout this time, Tyrone has accomplished goals away from the school building as well. He has published two children's books, *Bradley Knows Everything* and *Bradley Visits the Zoo*, which sees his son, Bradley, as the main character, and a coloring book entitled The Bradley Imagination Book. All books are available on Amazon. He has also been a featured speaker for various organizations and started a show surrounding fatherhood.

He speaks to students and kids as young as elementary students to college athletes. Tyrone has also created and presented multiple professional development programs to educators and corporations, surrounding topics such as relationship building, equity and diversity, and motivation, as well as fatherhood and literacy.

ABOUT THE LEAD AUTHOR

Chip Baker is a fourth-generation educator. He has been a teacher and coach for over twenty-two years. He is a multiple-time best-selling author, YouTuber, podcaster, motivational speaker, and life coach.

Chip Baker is the creator of the YouTube channel and podcast *Chip Baker—The Success Chronicles*, where he interviews people from all walks of life and shares their stories for positive inspiration and motivation.

Live. Learn. Serve. Inspire. Go get it!

Email: chipbakertsc@gmail.com
Online Store:
http://chip-baker-the-success-chronicles.square.site/
Facebook Page:
https://www.facebook.com/profile.php?id=100014641035295
Instagram: @chipbakertsc
LinkedIn:
http://linkedin.com/in/chip-baker-thesuccesschronicles-825887161
Twitter: @chipbaker19

Chip Baker—The Success Chronicles

YouTube: youtube.com/c/ChipBakerTheSuccessChronicles
Podcast: https://anchor.fm/chip-baker

Other Books:
Growing Through Your Go Through
Effective Conversation to Ignite Relationships
Suited for Success, Vol. 2
The Formula Chart for Life
The Impact of Influence Vol. 1,2, & 3
R.O.C.K. Solid
Stay on the Right Path
Black Men Love

PICK UP THESE OTHER TITLES BY CHIP BAKER

 **GROWING THROUGH YOUR GO THROUGH**

 **EFFECTIVE CONVERSATION TO IGNITE RELATIONSHIP**

 SUITED FOR SUCCESS: VOLUME 2

 THE FORMULA CHART FOR LIFE

 THE IMPACT OF INFLUENCE: VOLUME 1

 THE IMPACT OF INFLUENCE: VOLUME 2

 **R.O.C.K. SOLID**

 STAY ON THE RIGHT P.A.T.H.

 **THE IMPACT OF INFLUENCE: VOLUME 3**

 **BLACK MEN LOVE**

To order your autographed copies visit
http://chip-baker-the-success-chronicles.square.site/